DEATH TO THE BCS

DEATH TO THE BCS

**The Definitive Case Against
the Bowl Championship Series**

**DAN WETZEL,
JOSH PETER, AND JEFF PASSAN**

GOTHAM BOOKS

GOTHAM BOOKS
Published by Penguin Group (USA) Inc.
375 Hudson Street, New York, New York 10014, U.S.A.
Penguin Group (Canada), 90 Eglinton Avenue East, Suite 700, Toronto, Ontario M4P 2Y3,
Canada (a division of Pearson Penguin Canada Inc.); Penguin Books Ltd, 80 Strand, London
WC2R 0RL, England; Penguin Ireland, 25 St Stephen's Green, Dublin 2, Ireland (a division of
Penguin Books Ltd); Penguin Group (Australia), 250 Camberwell Road, Camberwell, Victoria
3124, Australia (a division of Pearson Australia Group Pty Ltd); Penguin Books India Pvt Ltd,
11 Community Centre, Panchsheel Park, New Delhi – 110 017, India; Penguin Group (NZ), 67
Apollo Drive, Rosedale, North Shore 0632, New Zealand (a division of Pearson New Zealand
Ltd); Penguin Books (South Africa) (Pty) Ltd, 24 Sturdee Avenue, Rosebank, Johannesburg
2196, South Africa

Penguin Books Ltd, Registered Offices: 80 Strand, London WC2R 0RL, England

Published by Gotham Books, a member of Penguin Group (USA) Inc.

First printing, October 2010
10 9 8 7 6 5 4 3 2

Gotham Books and the skyscraper logo are trademarks of Penguin Group (USA) Inc.

LIBRARY OF CONGRESS CATALOGING-IN-PUBLICATION DATA
Wetzel, Dan.
   Death to the BCS : the definitive case against the Bowl Championship Series / by Dan
Wetzel, Josh Peter, and Jeff Passan.
      p.   cm.
   ISBN 978–1–592–40570–1 (hardcover)
   1. Bowl Championship Series—Corrupt practices.   2. College sports—Corrupt practices—
United States.   3. BCS National Championship Game (Football game).   4. Football—Corrupt
practices—United States.   I. Peter, Josh.   II. Passan, Jeff.   III. Title.
   GV959.W47 2010
   796.332'63—dc22   2010029575

Printed in the United States of America
Set in Apollo MT Std
Designed by Sabrina Bowers

To our families, for whom the BCS can't die soon enough

CONTENTS

DEATH TO THE
BCS

INTRODUCTION
The Cartel

For two years, we pored over thousands of pages of tax filings, university contracts, and congressional testimony. We criss-crossed the country interviewing the pertinent power players in college football, on and off the record. We filed dozens of Freedom of Information requests. We wanted to answer one question: Why is college football *really* saddled with the brain-dead Bowl Championship Series? We sought the truth because tens of millions of fans deserve it.

We discovered an ocean of corruption: sophisticated scams, mind-numbing waste, and naked political deals—enough to prove that the confused excuses spat out by the suits in charge and regurgitated by their well-paid public relations people are empty drivel. While the sleaze should be enough to cause the death of the BCS, it's simply emblematic of a long battle best represented by two men. One stands for common sense and the possibilities the great game can offer. The other is about protecting the one-sided system that enriches and empowers the very few who led college football into this morass, even as it runs counter to their teams' competitive interests.

You've heard of the first. His name is Joe Paterno. He's the eighty-three-year-old icon who, after sixty-one seasons coaching at Penn State, the last forty-five as head coach, is as steadfast a proponent of a playoff as ever. He is us. He is you. He is everyone whose gag reflex engages upon the mere thought of how college football crowns its national champion.

You might not have heard of the other. His name is Jim Delany. He's the balding, sixty-two-year-old former assistant district attorney who is the commissioner of Penn State's conference, the Big Ten. He is one of the most powerful people in college athletics. His influence far outweighs that of even the NCAA president, because Delany belongs to the group that hijacked college football and refuses to let go.

Paterno may be the king of the sport, but Delany is the ayatollah, speaking the word of God.

And that word is no.

No to a playoff. No to an extra championship game following the bowl season. No to any semblance of sanity in America's greatest spectator sport. No to anything but the loathsome, odious, reviled BCS.

For twelve years, the BCS has decided the national champion at the highest level of college football, Division I-A. Two human polls and one computer ranking combine to determine the two teams that play in the BCS National Championship Game. Other top-ranked teams go to the BCS-supported Rose Bowl, Sugar Bowl, Orange Bowl, and Fiesta Bowl. Delany helped run the BCS amid widespread skepticism. It's been a bigger disaster than anyone could have imagined. Its approval rating hovers around 10 percent. And yet Delany draws the following conclusion: "It's been incredibly successful."

For him and his cronies, sure. The BCS is a group of similar businesses that bands together in search of money and power, harming the public along the way. It gives off a wretched smell— that of a cartel. While a labor lawyer might disagree on the word's usage, it fits for the BCS power brokers: Rather than jack up gas prices or cut off the oil supply like OPEC can, the college football Cartel controls the postseason and the revenue it generates while pretending a playoff would put at risk something as sacred as the history and tradition of the Papajohns.com Bowl.

Officially, the BCS is run by twelve men: the commissioners of major college football's eleven conferences and the athletic director of Notre Dame. Realistically, six men control college football: the commissioners of the Atlantic Coast, Big East, Big Ten, Big 12, Pac-10, and Southeastern conferences. They squirrel away the sport's revenues, crush any challenge to their supremacy, and make decision after ill-fated decision that takes college football eons further from what its fans want.

Alongside Delany, Mike Slive (SEC), Dan Beebe (Big 12), John Swofford (ACC), Larry Scott (Pac-10), and John Marinatto (Big East) guide the BCS to a place where their conferences receive automatic bids to the BCS games with massive payouts. This is college football's Cartel.

While the big six conferences hogged 82.3 percent of the $155.2 million paid out by BCS games last year, the Mountain West Conference, Western Athletic Conference, Mid-American Conference, Conference USA, and Sun Belt Conference scraped along with the leftovers. The Cartel and the BCS exist to consolidate control among the power conferences and position themselves to never let go. Suggesting a playoff to the Cartel is futile because it doesn't care how big the postseason revenue pie gets or even if its slice would grow. It simply wants to ensure that no one else holds the knife.

The six Cartel members work with a legion of henchmen—the executive directors of a couple dozen bowl games and a few high-powered athletic directors and school presidents—to dictate how the sport operates. Formally, the Cartel doesn't exist. Neither, for that matter, does the BCS. It's not a legal construct, just a series of contracts among various entities, which makes it hard for opponents to trace it, sue it, or pin it down. As much as some government officials would love to bust it using the Sherman Antitrust Act before the current BCS television deals run out in 2014—the Justice Department announced in January that it might open an investigation—the case is not a certain winner, even if the BCS seems so patently wrong.

Five teams finished the 2009 regular season with perfect records. Since the BCS exists to provide a title game between the two teams it deems best—and, more often than not, the results are controversial thanks to flawed ranking systems—the other three undefeated teams were left with consolation matchups. This is not the best way to determine a national champion as much as a get-rich, stay-rich scheme carried out at the expense of fairness, taxpayers, and college football fans.

"It has given the commissioners power and significance," said Gene Bleymaier, the athletic director at Boise State University. "Prior to this, conference commissioners had very little power. No one knew them. They had very little significance outside of their conference."

Paterno is too old to care about perceived power. He wants what's fair, and that is a playoff. Four times he led Penn State to undefeated seasons and didn't win a national championship. Perhaps no other person has been so wronged by the lack of a proper postseason. It may be the only issue where Paterno is considered a forward-thinking revolutionary. Paterno translated the *Aeneid* from Latin to English in high school and said the epic poem guides his coaching style. He claimed he has neither sent nor read an e-mail in his life. When the NCAA imposed legislation that limited coaches sending text messages to recruits, he was baffled.

"I thought it was tech messaging—T-E-C-H," Paterno told the *New York Times*.

Paterno knew how to use the phone, and one particular day

the lack of a playoff so aggrieved him that he called Delany. Paterno didn't hold back. The Cartel can make anything happen in college football, and even Paterno, a man who loathes change, understood college football needed it. Delany told Paterno the university presidents with the power to change the system were pro-BCS. Paterno insisted the presidents would follow wherever Delany led. Delany didn't budge. The call ended without resolution. Nothing would change.

The Cartel doesn't just laugh at Joe Paterno. It laughs at you, too. The joke is on fans who dream of college football finding a postseason worthy of its pageantry. Even the leader of the free world is beyond its reach. In November 2008, President-elect Barack Obama declared the sport needed a playoff. Delany treated the president of the United States the same way he does every challenger to his monopoly: He dismissed him. "I think it's that time of year," he told Pete Thamel of the *New York Times*.

The Cartel entrenched itself through a campaign that spreads misinformation and perpetuates falsehoods. Debate about how to fix college football is ill-informed and often dizzies the participants. This is exactly how the powers that be want it. By shrouding the most important part of their sport in confusion and mystery, and by tossing out phony arguments and distracting canards, and even by having spokesmen obfuscate not just to the public but to Congress, the Cartel has so waylaid college football that even a do-anything spirit like Joe Paterno throws his hands up in defeat.

Fortunately, we know a few things Paterno doesn't.

We know how the BCS really works, or, more accurately, doesn't work. It's every bit as troubling as the old coach can imagine. Because of the BCS, universities have blown nearly $2 million paying for empty seats at a single game. Because of the BCS, athletic directors cash $30,000-plus bonus checks, even for sending teams to the lowliest of bowl games. Because of the BCS, teams are rewarded for waltzing through cupcake schedules every fall. Because of the BCS, Division I-A college football is the only sport in which the NCAA declines to crown an official national champion.

There is no smoking gun with the BCS. The BCS *is* the smoking gun.

The bowl system, the foundation of the BCS, is a mess, which is a shame. We love bowl games. The major ones and the little ones, the unusual matchups, the crazy comebacks, the nothing-to-lose finishes. How the Independence Bowl in Shreveport, Louisiana, and the Sun Bowl in El Paso, Texas, still mean something to their communities. While critics cry about too many bowls, we disagree. More football is never a bad thing.

Except that disease has infiltrated the bowl's circulatory system, pumping from the heart all the way to the tiniest veins. The power-conference commissioners scheme to protect their dominant position in the postseason. The bowl executives rake in huge salaries while serving as middlemen. Nearly 60 percent of schools spend more money to participate in bowls than the games offer in payouts.

The outdated bowl system blocks progress with its white-knuckle grip on the sport. Forget the month of football nirvana a playoff would provide. Today, the schools lose, the fans lose, and the sport itself loses. Doesn't matter, because the suits win, quite handsomely, and to defend the indefensible they resort to bad arguments, anything to quiet the constant din for a playoff.

"How would band members, cheerleaders, and other students make holiday plans knowing their team might play one, two, or three games on campus during the time they are normally home with their families?" BCS executive director Bill Hancock asked.

Apparently, inconvenienced cheerleaders are a prime defense for the BCS. Such rationale comes as much from hubris as foolhardiness. The BCS treats college football fans like they're stupid. It takes credit for the rise in the sport's popularity, comparing today's title game to the mess of split championships that preceded it. It's like trying to say a busted calculator is good because it's newer than an abacus.

The system isn't merely broken, either. It is smashed, crushed, twisted, and mangled, totaled beyond belief, and there is no fixing it. College football needs to start over. Only, the Cartel won't budge, not when it has the power, which, in this case, it deems more valuable than the additional cash a playoff would create.

And it's a lot of money. An awful lot. Experts estimate a college football playoff could approach $750 million in annual revenue, more than $600 million ahead of the current system. The old bowls would survive mostly as is, no matter what dire predictions the Cartel repeats. Run in concert with the playoff, they would generate another $100 million-plus in gross revenues. As tuition rises to obscene levels, endowments dry up, donations plummet, and schools look for taxpayer subsidies, the BCS bosses continue to sit on a diamond mine because they so relish their position.

Without NCAA oversight and no impartial official looking out for the welfare of all 120 schools, the BCS honchos act like the worst of our politicians, more concerned with spending riders and petty pork projects than what's best for the nation. Among the Cartel there is a lack of comity and commonality, a stark contrast to its sport, which every Saturday beams with tens of thousands of people at historic on-campus stadiums sharing passion and memories and beer and the dream of a playoff.

There is a grassroots groundswell that threatens the establishment. Already Boise State and the University of Utah, up-start programs from smaller conferences, have penetrated the BCS and won major bowl games over big-name opponents. The victories only steeled the Cartel. While Utah gained an invitation to the Pac-10 beginning in 2011, the system didn't change. Championship access means money, and money could turn the Boise States and TCUs of the world into annual powerhouses. Soon enough people might start asking why the six major conferences get to call the shots. The control of money, then, is sacrosanct, far more than the promise of underdogs slaying historic programs, of games in December and January climaxing with a real championship, of March Madness–level excitement in a football playoff.

So for now the BCS survives, a roach amid a typhoon of Raid, emanating coldness, ignoring the measured consideration of old coaching icons, and dismissing fans' bellows. Even the unyielding push of common sense is held off with mistruths and misdirection that turn the entire issue into a river of red herrings.

Facts have power, though. The truth has might. The rational presentation of both can upend even the longest-held conventional wisdom and expose the Cartel for what it is: a not-half-as-smart-as-it-wants-you-to-believe group of leaders that history will one day mock for its obstinacy.

To properly dismantle the BCS, we need to start by defining a suitable alternative. An argument against something is hollow without a superior substitute. So before we get to the goriest details of everything wrong with the BCS, we'll take you through all that's right with our playoff plan, something that would stand on its own even without the BCS serving as a sham of a solution.

"The single most frustrating notion is, 'We understand it's

not perfect, but it's the best we can do,'" Mountain West commissioner Craig Thompson said. "That's just irritating. There are a lot of smart people, creative people."

In seeking the optimal playoff plan, we did something the Cartel would never dare: We talked with those smart, creative people—conference commissioners, marketing professionals, athletic directors, television executives, economists, professors, bowl representatives, NFL executives, and more. They brainstormed, hypothesized, planned, and ruminated, and together it came, an impermeable idea whose lone impediment is six men and the control they refuse to cede.

What follows is no fantasy, no wild theory, no pipe dream that's alive only in some heavenly place where Woody Hayes and Bear Bryant are coaching against each other. It's tangible and feasible, and it benefits every TV entity, every university, every player, every coach, and especially every fan.

This is what a real playoff looks like.

1 The Plan

There are three chief criteria for a playoff plan to work:

1. It must be more profitable in every imaginable way for colleges and universities.
2. It must protect, if not increase, the value of the regular season.
3. It must take academics into consideration, if only so presidents can save face for their long-standing hypocrisy on the issue.

The Cartel seems to want playoff proponents to argue about the right plan because the greater the variety of proposals out there, the easier it is to dismiss them all as the confused ram blings of uninformed outsiders. They desire the devil to be in the details. And with tens of millions of angry fans, there is no shortage of ideas. Unfortunately, most are unworkable.

First, let's get rid of the nonstarters: Any plan that includes dropping regular-season games, eliminating conference championship games, realigning leagues, or using bowl games as host sites for playoff games could never pass muster with most schools. The Cartel knows as much. Those are exactly the kind of doomed plans it wants pushed forward.

This is the opposite, bold yet realistic. Even the staunchest Cartel members have difficulty arguing against it. Former Pac-10 commissioner Tom Hansen, among the most hardcore BCS backers past and present, has said the model we use is the only acceptable option.

Our plan for Division I-A football: a sixteen-team playoff that provides automatic bids for all eleven conference champions and at-large slots for five remaining teams. Yes, all eleven conference champions, even the lousy ones, determined through traditional means: either the regular season or conference-title games, which would continue unabated. While no one would argue that the Sun Belt champ is one of the top sixteen teams in the country, its presence is paramount to maintaining the integrity and relevancy of the regular season. It creates incentive for regular-season success.

The best teams earn the highest seeds and are rewarded with home games for the first three rounds. The championship game is held at a neutral site. The No. 1 seed doesn't just get rewarded with the weakest opponent—in most years the Sun Belt champion—but the ensuing rounds on its home field. Finish fifth and face a first-round battle against a No. 12 seed likely from a power conference, then a second-round game on the road. The difference between first and fifth is significant.

By playing games on campus, the tournament would also include what is perhaps the best part of college football: its historic stadiums and game-day environments. There's no good reason to conduct playoff games in sterile, often-under-capacity crowds at municipal stadiums in far-off cities when the incomparable feeling of The Swamp in Gainesville, The Horseshoe in Columbus, or the Coliseum in Los Angeles beckons.

Suddenly, the top seeds' squaring off against small-conference competition doesn't lend itself to fan apathy. Devotees would pack their home stadiums, and television viewers would be treated to the Cinderella possibility college football so sorely lacks.

The men's basketball tournament is successful because in early games little schools dare to dream, and the Final Four allows heavyweight programs to determine who is best. That combination creates incredible drama, draws in casual fans, and delivers the television ratings that generate billions of dollars. Perhaps the Mid-American Conference champion would never win this playoff, but the possibility that a MAC team could—not to mention the likelihood that soon enough, a high seed will be upset in the first round—portends magic.

A small selection committee, such as the one used for the men's basketball tournament, would determine the five at-large bids. Dealing with set and specific criteria, the committee can make informed decisions and eliminate confused poll voters and mathematically dubious computer formulas from the equation. Arguments over the final spots and seeding would happen just as they do with berths to BCS bowls, only the arguments would center on which two-loss team was left out, not which unbeaten school missed its shot at the championship. Besides, debates are never a bad thing in sports—unless they're nonsensical, like whether something so flawed as the BCS is a proper way to determine college football's champion.

Competition for the five at-large spots would make the final month of the regular season a circus of action, playoff chances coming and going with each touchdown, excitement saturating the country. It would compel Pac-10 fans to follow the Big East, SEC fans to pay attention to the Mountain West, ACC fans to study up on the Western Athletic Conference. TV ratings would jump. The Internet would buckle from excitement. Any team, big or small, independent or affiliated, would be eligible for an at-large bid. Notre Dame and the service academies could gain entry with one of the five extra slots.

To see what could've been, view the chart on the following page: Our sixteen-team playoff in 2009, with the higher seeds hosting games until the championship.

The entire playoff would be conducted over four weekends,

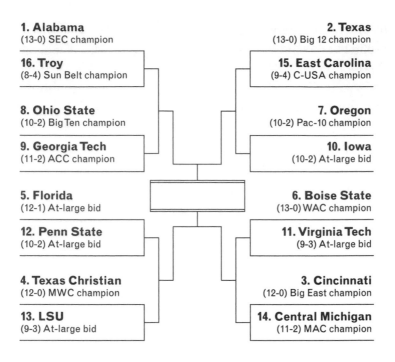

1. Alabama
(13-0) SEC champion

2. Texas
(13-0) Big 12 champion

16. Troy
(8-4) Sun Belt champion

15. East Carolina
(9-4) C-USA champion

8. Ohio State
(10-2) Big Ten champion

7. Oregon
(10-2) Pac-10 champion

9. Georgia Tech
(11-2) ACC champion

10. Iowa
(10-2) At-large bid

5. Florida
(12-1) At-large bid

6. Boise State
(13-0) WAC champion

12. Penn State
(10-2) At-large bid

11. Virginia Tech
(9-3) At-large bid

4. Texas Christian
(12-0) MWC champion

3. Cincinnati
(12-0) Big East champion

13. LSU
(9-3) At-large bid

14. Central Michigan
(11-2) MAC champion

the same time frame in which the current bowl schedule operates. The playoff would allow a two- to three-week break for final exams for student athletes, then kick off the weekend before Christmas and conclude the second Monday of January. In 2011, that's the same date as the BCS title game. At most, two teams would play seventeen games, which is one more than some high school state champions.

Bowls would go nowhere—and certainly not out of business, as the Cartel wants you to believe. They would have no role in the playoff but continue to provide non-playoff teams a chance for a postseason game. This would allow college football to end the most illogical business arrangement in all of sports: outsourcing its most profitable product, postseason football. The bowl system, a consolidation of private businesses with no official ties to universities, sucks tens of millions of dollars in profit away from schools. With on-campus games, the money stays within college athletics.

And the money. Oh, the money. The playoff plan is a legal bank heist, a design that would endow the schools rather than burgle them. It would make the BCS payouts look like a pittance. Even the Cartel admits that.

"I am absolutely sure that an NFL-style football playoff would provide maybe three or four times as many dollars . . . than the present system does," Delany said before Congress in 2005.

The current bowl system pays college football about $220 million in gross revenue per year. After the schools pick up the cost of travel, tickets, and bonuses, they walk with $140 million in profit.

Delany's projection of a potential $880 million gross is in line with our experts' estimate: $750 million a year for the playoff alone. Each of the fifteen games would pay out $25 million per team. Yes, a first-round playoff game would net conferences 40 percent more than the current BCS championship game.

Even after serious cuts to television revenue, our panel concluded, the bowl system could still pay out 50 percent of its current rate, or $110 million. Combined, there's an $860 million postseason waiting to be tapped, an unheard of sum in amateur athletics. It's the kind of money that makes tradition-crippling conference expansion unnecessary.

As the Cartel yammers on about its system being not just the right way but the only way, this playoff plan shows otherwise—and it's just the beginning. The pile of evidence against the BCS stretches to the moon, and the foundation of every Cartel argument is made of quicksand.

It's not like we're playoff-design geniuses. What preceded was essentially the model the NCAA uses to run football championships in Division I-AA, Division II, and Division III. (The official term for Division I-AA these days is Football Championship Subdivision, while Division I-A is called Football Bowl Subdivision. We refuse, out of principle, to bother with such silly names. We're hopelessly old-school.) While the NCAA has its flaws, there is no denying its skill at running national tournaments. It does so with great success and excitement in eighty-eight different sports and divisions in everything from men's basketball to riflery. Only in one sport does the NCAA not crown an official champion: Division I-A football.

The association's central office has no power or jurisdiction over major college football's postseason. Officially, the NCAA treats the glass football held by the winning coach after the BCS championship game like it does the stemware on its table: just another piece of crystal.

Delany, Slive, and the others participate in high-level committees that make NCAA policy on all things except the college football postseason, then step outside their NCAA roles, don their BCS hats, and run that, too. Confused? Everyone is. Former NCAA president Cedric Dempsey used to shake his head at the annual deluge of angry mail he'd receive about the BCS, something over which he wielded no power. This is exactly how the Cartel wants it. Blame the other guy, the wrong guy, and engage in subterfuge while the perfect plan is waiting to be implemented.

"Advocates of a hypothetical playoff can't agree on how to resolve key playoff questions: who, what, where, and when," BCS executive director Bill Hancock said.

Since we've answered each of those, we might as well ask another question: How? By exposing the fraudulence that defines the Cartel to its very last fiber.

2 What Could Have Been

Vince Dooley felt a sense of conviction and hope. It was May 1994, and he arrived at the Southeastern Conference meetings at the Hilton Sandestin Beach Golf Resort & Spa with a solution to college football's postseason problem. Awaiting him in a conference room was a group of fellow power brokers that had a choice: help thrust college football into the future, or maintain the broken status quo.

Dooley greeted them and set up a slide presentation. During his twenty-five seasons as football coach at the University of Georgia, he had established himself as one of the sport's most respected figures. He amassed more influence after taking over as Georgia's athletic director. Dooley knew both the game of college football and the business of college football. He wasn't a crusader as much as a pragmatist, and he hoped the compelling case on those slides would appeal to his fellow SEC athletic directors at their annual get-together in Destin, Florida.

Seven months earlier, the NCAA had formed a high-level committee to study a playoff. Chaired by UCLA chancellor Charles Young, the group looked at every possible facet of a playoff: academic concerns, weather patterns, television schedules. It emerged with a several-hundred-page-long report that it presented to a twenty-five-member panel of football and business royalty that included Dooley. Ideas ranged from a single-game national championship to a sixteen-team playoff. The playoff options would generate a huge influx of cash, which was critical for the majority of schools that depended on football revenue to fund their athletic departments. For the playoff to become a reality, it needed the approval of key stakeholders.

Dooley was an ideal agent for change, and armed with slides that sketched a workable playoff plan, his hope was to bring the SEC on board. He outlined that day a proposal that would preserve the bowl system and create three additional games— two semifinal matchups and a national championship. The plan called for the four teams to be selected after the January 1 bowl games.

As much sense as it made then and still does nearly two decades later, the playoff plan never had a chance. And Dooley realized as much shortly after his presentation ended. He may have won 201 games and a national championship, may have coached Herschel Walker, and may have become a football icon throughout the South, but Dooley was no match for the man who truly ruled the room: Roy Kramer, the commissioner of the SEC.

"I think we'll have another option," Dooley recalled Kramer saying cryptically.

While Dooley had been working with the NCAA's committee, Kramer had helped orchestrate secret negotiations with commissioners of the five other conferences that eventually formed the core of the Cartel and the BCS. To say that the NCAA's appeal to fair play faced a tough crowd when Dooley presented the playoff plan in that Hilton conference room is an understatement.

The conference commissioners had filled the leadership void in college football, and Kramer was the alpha dog. SEC football under Kramer was as cutthroat as the sport has ever been. During his run as commissioner from 1990 to 2002, he pioneered such groundbreaking and profitable ideas as expanding the league to twelve teams and creating the conference champion-ship game. He piloted the conference during an era of rampant rule-breaking that kept the NCAA infractions committee busy, with all twelve SEC athletic departments racking up at least one major violation conviction during his tenure.

The ACC, Big Ten, Big 12, Big East, Pac-10, and SEC—the six so-called equity conferences that comprised the ruling class of college athletics—didn't object to the concept of a four-team playoff as much as they hated the idea of ceding control to the NCAA. The bowl system allowed equity conferences to hoard more than 85 percent of the postseason revenue. The NCAA-run men's basketball tournament resulted in a slightly more equita-ble distribution of postseason revenue based on performance, and to a group guided by avarice, such a thing was unacceptable. If the league commissioners were in charge, though, they could guarantee that they controlled access to the bowls.

No one debated that a four-team playoff would generate tens of millions of dollars in additional money or that the revenue shares initially would remain similar. It stood to reason that the only participants in the four-team playoff would come from big conferences, because it's not like Sun Belt Conference teams were cracking the top 20, let alone the top 4. Fear of the unknown and unforeseen, of an uprising among the smaller schools, prompted the equity conferences to follow the lead of so many in positions of power: use strength to squash the minority.

"I don't want to say that Roy and the commissioners were thinking only of the equity part of it," Dooley said. "But it was certainly, obviously, a motivating factor."

Less than two weeks after Dooley's doomed presentation in Florida, Kramer and his cohorts unveiled the precursor of the BCS. The Bowl Alliance, they called it, and the system relied on the same old polls and the same old bowls as part of an attempt to match the Nos. 1 and 2 teams. The NCAA promptly tabled the idea of a four-team playoff. It amounted to surrender.

The Bowl Alliance started in 1995 without the Big Ten and Pac-10, whose refusal to join was, of course, a self-serving reflex. The conferences were determined to protect their lucrative arrangement with the Rose Bowl. Yet in 1998, after they saw an opportunity to make more money through capitulation, the Big Ten and Pac-10 dumped their exclusive agreement with the Rose Bowl. Turns out tradition did have a price. Thus was born the Bowl Championship Series. And to the chagrin of the fans, coaches, and players who seek progress, the Cartel was entrenched.

More than a decade later it remains so, as does its flawed postseason. In the face of compelling evidence against its utility, the BCS engages in revisionist history trying to defend itself. The argument goes that while the BCS may not be perfect, it was the most perfect option at the time. It wasn't, of course, or Dooley would not have clicked from slide to slide in Destin. At that crucial moment in 1994, the Cartel actively chose a flawed BCS over a playoff.

Inaccurate history, confused facts, and unnecessary hyperbole are the bread and butter of the Cartel. To this day, it argues that a playoff is too confusing to run and falsely claims no one has put forth a legitimate playoff plan.

"Playoff advocates have had an easy ride where they have never been called on to explain exactly how they would create an alternative," Ari Fleischer, the former press secretary for President George W. Bush, told Politico.com when he was hired by the Cartel as a public-relations consultant in 2009.

Never any alternatives? Well, there was the NCAA's exhaustive report and Dooley's presentation in 1994. And a $3 billion offer in 1999 from a Swiss group to stage a sixteen-team playoff. Plus the joint SEC-ACC "plus-one" proposal in 2008 outlining an extra championship game after bowl season. And the lengthy eight-team playoff plan the Mountain West Conference authored in 2009. Don't forget the myriad detailed systems drawn up through the years by athletic directors, private businessmen, and even the president of the University of Georgia.

Fleischer managed to have it backward when he claimed playoff proponents have had a free ride. It's the BCS that has sailed along by not having to defend against a specific plan that all fans understand. The disorganization of the playoff crowd created the sort of gridlock in which the Cartel specializes.

3 Obstruction of Justice

Every cartel needs protection, and so May 1, 2009, on Capitol Hill, the BCS unleashed its version. It wasn't a crooked cop or a corrupt government, like the world's others employ. It wasn't even a smooth-talking, Brioni-suit-wearing lawyer with a six-figure retainer. This Cartel trotted out a bumbling bowl executive who, within minutes of introducing himself to Congress, may have committed perjury.

Derrick Fox, the CEO of the Alamo Bowl, was the Cartel's choice to stand next to ACC commissioner John Swofford in front of a House Energy and Commerce subcommittee. Fox's job was to swear to tell the truth, the whole truth and nothing but the truth —and convince the nation that a college football playoff is a very bad idea.

A playoff would be catastrophic to any bowl executive, so Fox wanted to persuade Congress that deviating from the BCS carried an inherent and irreparable risk. It was a classic scare tactic, and he employed artifice because the truth was too damaging. Bowl-game profits siphon as much as 40 percent of college football's postseason revenue, money that could replace tax dollars in balancing public schools' athletic-department budgets. The desire of bowl executives to maintain huge salaries and cushy jobs stands in the way of a playoff worth hundreds of millions of additional dollars to the universities. And even though a playoff would cut into revenue, bowls would still survive—just not with the excess riches and prestige to which bowl executives are accustomed.

With such bleakness staring at him, Fox pulled the oratory version of a fumblerooski. He didn't declare that bowl games are mere football contests. No, in the world of the Cartel, they are altruistic endeavors that just happen to involve a bunch of kids playing football.

"Almost all the postseason bowl games are put on by charitable groups, and since up to one-quarter of the proceeds from the games are dedicated to the community, local charities received tens of millions of dollars a year," Fox said.

His thirty-eight words contained three outrageous exaggerations, which, even for Washington, may be a record. Rep. Joe Barton (R-Texas), who chaired the hearings, would later say the comments possibly qualified as "perjury" and "contempt of Congress."

Fox's claims sounded good. No one is against charity. Kill a bowl game, run by some bare-bones, benevolent group, and a poor, homeless child might starve outside a soup kitchen the next winter. It was a line of reasoning that would cause a politician to pause and the public, which would read the unchecked comments in news accounts, to see the pro-bowl argument in a new light.

Tax documents and other public records document a much different reality.

Take exaggeration No. 1: "Almost all the postseason bowl games are put on by charitable groups . . ."

Actually, not a single bowl game is run by a group that could be described as a charity under any commonsense definition. The bowls are controlled, in fact, by executive directors who make fabulous coin, treat their business cronies to lavish swag, and celebrate their altogether awesome lives with righteous parties. You know, just like Mother Teresa did.

Eight of the thirty-five bowl games scheduled for this year are privately owned, six of them by ESPN. So nearly a quarter of bowl games are the opposite of charities. They exist purely and expressly for profit. They even pay taxes.

Reached after his testimony, Fox would not budge. He claimed a multinational corporation such as ESPN, whose parent, The Walt Disney Company, did $37.8 billion in revenue in 2008, does indeed qualify as a charitable group.

"Well," Fox said, "[Walt Disney is] certainly involved in charitable activities."

It doesn't end there. The remaining twenty-seven bowls aren't run by charities, either. They simply enjoy 501(c)(3) not-for-profit status from the Internal Revenue Service, which allows them to avoid paying federal, state, and local taxes. It's a sweetheart deal.

Not-for-profit is a misnomer of sorts. It doesn't mean there is zero profit involved. It's merely an accounting term for an organization mainly devoted to a public purpose that does not distribute its surplus—often vast—to owners or shareholders. Since no specific person or company owns the bowl games, no one can sell them or walk away with tens of millions of dollars. In the meantime, however, those in charge can drain every last penny of revenue out of the not-for-profit. Unspent revenue goes into reserves, where it can be tapped later. Not-for-profits of all kinds are known to spend lavishly on employees, facilities, and programs, the antithesis of the poor, struggling charity the term conjures.

Harvard University, for instance, is the oldest corporation in the United States, founded in 1636 and incorporated in 1650. Yet it enjoys not-for-profit status despite having total assets of

$43.8 billion, according to fiscal 2008 tax filings. That includes an endowment of nearly $37 billion. It charges undergraduates nearly $50,000 a year in tuition, fees, and housing. Massachusetts politicians have attacked Harvard for not having to pay taxes on its considerable investments.

It's no different for bowl games. Major bowl games have major investment portfolios ($34.6 million for the Sugar Bowl), which most years can easily produce millions in returns. Not having to pay taxes on that investment income (hundreds of thousands and even millions of dollars) allows bowl directors an extra revenue stream to cover high salaries, unnecessary costs, and general mismanagement.

In the case of bowl games, not-for-profit status isn't something that should elicit sympathy. It's a benefit that helps assure their affluent existence.

As for Fox's "charity" line, while nearly all charities—say, the American Cancer Society or the Salvation Army—are non-profits, not all nonprofits are charities. To imply so, as Fox did under oath in front of Congress, smacks of manipulative double-speak and opportunism.

"You've got to remember, when you're looking at nonprofit [bowl games] there really is a difference [from] a United Way," said Jim McVay, CEO of the Outback Bowl, when told of Fox's statement. "There's a difference in economics."

In other words, calling them "almost all" charities might score emotional points with meddling lawmakers and media. It just isn't the truth.

Fox was just getting started. Exaggeration No. 2—". . . up to one-quarter of the proceeds from the games are dedicated to the community . . ."—was a whopper.

Before we get to what bowl games give—and it's frighteningly little—let's start with what they take. The twenty-three games with records publicly available received $7.5 million in direct government handouts, according to their federal tax filings. That's straight cash. It doesn't factor in the estimated millions from police and fire department detail work, traffic control, clean up, and other public services donated to the games by local governments that assume the overtime costs.

The Sugar Bowl, for instance, received $3 million in direct funding from the Louisiana state government, according to its 2008 tax filing, the most recent made public. The government gravy train is so important to the Sugar Bowl that the game pays a lobbying firm in Baton Rouge to ensure its public financing.

With the bowl receiving so much, then, it stands to reason that what Fox considers a charitable group would reciprocate the giving. The organization brought in $34.1 million in revenue in fiscal 2007, according to its most recent federal 990 tax form. One quarter of that, per Fox's testimony, would be about $8.525 million.

The Sugar Bowl gave nothing. Not a buck to the Hurricane Katrina reconstruction effort. Not a dime to a New Orleans after-school program. Not a penny to Habitat for Humanity. The Sugar Bowl, one of the richest bowls in existence, didn't give back 25 percent of its proceeds to the community. It hogged everything, including the $3 million in taxpayers' money.

In a purely semantic way, Fox was right. The Sugar Bowl did fall into the category of "up to one-quarter." Just at the opposite end of the spectrum. "Zero is not the impression I got," Barton said.

It's not like the Sugar Bowl lacked money to give. The $34.1 million in revenue was offset by just $22.5 million in expenses, so it turned an $11.6 million, tax-free profit. It ended the fiscal year with $37 million in assets. Which is necessary since the Sugar Bowl's checkbook is a sieve everywhere else.

Executive director Paul Hoolahan received $607,500 in total compensation in fiscal 2008, according to its tax return. Associate executive director Jeff Hundley took in $375,732. Three other employees averaged $118,663 in total compensation.

Don't forget the lifestyle that comes with outrageous expense accounts, travel budgets, and a bank account padded annually by the state. The following expenditures are real. They come from the Sugar Bowl's tax returns from 2005, '06, and '07:

- $494,177 on "entertainment" (2005)
- $455,781 on "special appropriations" (2006)
- $188,305 on "Hall of Fame" (2005)
- $201,226 on "gifts and bonuses" (2007)
- $684,578 on "media relations" (2007)
- $330,244 on "decorations" (2007)
- $114,666 on "committee meetings" (2006)
- $46,017 on "conference meetings" (2006)
- $91,983 on "conference relations" (2007)
- $58,995 on "liaison" (2006)
- $158,030 on "Allstate (Insurance) liaison" (2007)
- $447,817 on "Sugar Bowl event-related entertainment" (2007)
- $810,833 on "BCS Championship event-related entertainment" (2007)
- $82,884 on "other expenses" (2006)
- $260,062 on "other expenses" (2007)

On and on it goes. The Sugar Bowl has an actual "committee on golf" and a "special subcommittee on ladies' entertainment"— which may or may not have anything to do with all those liaisons.

All of this is completely legal. The Sugar Bowl can spend its money any way it wants. It can pay its people as much as it wants. It can buy as many decorations as it wants. Hoolahan is doing what every smart businessman would do—maximizing what is available to him. Look at the Music City Bowl. In 2003, bowl officials spent $7,203 on an office miniature golf tournament, according to the *Orange County Register*. Surely Tennesseans are thrilled to know the bowl that put on a nearly five-figure putt-putt match received upward of a half-million dollars in public funding since 2006.

As for exaggeration No. 3: ". . . local charities received tens of millions of dollars a year."

One look at the available records of the then twenty-three tax-exempt bowls (the Congressional Bowl was in its first year and had not filed), plus follow-up interviews with representatives of nearly every bowl, showed Fox wildly embellished the truth of the games' generosity.

The total payout to charities: a combined $3.2 million.

The bowls could give tens of millions of dollars a year; the tax-exempt bowls produced $186 million in revenue. And they combined to give just 1.7 percent of revenue to charity. Even worse, those bowls ended their fiscal years with $141 million in net assets, including more than $80 million in cash reserves.

"That doesn't seem like something that's really geared toward giving to charity, does it?" Rep. Barton said.

It seems like a calculated exaggeration meant to confuse Congress and the public. Barton didn't realize Fox's misrepresentation until informed by us soon after the testimony and long after the media dispersed the comments as fact.

Even fellow bowl executives couldn't defend Fox's claims. They know they aren't "charitable groups" no matter what Fox said under oath. They are under no obligation to give any money to charity, which is why most don't. More than half of the $3.2 million in charitable contributions came from just two bowl games, the Orange and the Chick-fil-A.

Others spread meager, largely symbolic donations around the area. The Florida Citrus Sports Association, which runs two Orlando-based games, donated just $10,570 of its $12.4 million in revenue to charities, according to its fiscal 2008 tax returns. One lucky recipient: the Pace Center for Girls, which received $120.

"If Derrick made that comment, that kind of invites, 'OK, let's go see how many tens of millions were involved here,'" said Hoolahan, the Sugar Bowl executive. "That sounds a little hyperbolic in the heat of battle."

Well, it came from a statement prepared in advance of the hearings. And Fox didn't back down in an interview, claiming his comments were fair and accurate, the information having been provided by the Football Bowl Association. In that phone conversation, Fox did concede it would be ridiculous to include as charitable donations the payouts bowl games make to participating teams. He later flip-flopped on that subject, telling media in San Antonio that bowl payouts should count as charitable contributions. By that logic, in Fox's world, Nick Saban and Mack Brown count as "local charities."

"To use the words 'local charities,' I assume it goes to the Boys & Girls Club, the YMCA," Barton said.

For his part, Swofford offered cover for the Cartel, using his stature as the ACC commissioner to support and praise Fox. (Swofford later declined our request to discuss his testimony.) If Swofford had an even cursory knowledge of bowl finances—and you'd suspect he does—he complied with Fox's exaggeration in triplicate.

"None of us in college football are anxious to jeopardize . . . the many . . . charitable endeavors undertaken by all of the bowl games," Swofford testified. He later added, ". . . the bowls and the host cities have been very good to the game. . . . They have been loyal supporters . . . and merit our full support."

The lawmakers weren't completely duped. Barton kept blasting away with critical questions and claiming that the BCS is "like communism. You can't fix it." Though he couldn't lie: The charitable stuff had sounded good at the time. No politician wanted to filch money from a local cause.

While some in Washington have wised up to the Cartel, the bowls have continued to operate below board with little recourse. The *Arizona Republic* reported in December 2009 that Fiesta Bowl employees were encouraged by executive director John Junker to make "contributions to politicians friendly to the bowl" and were later "reimbursed by the bowl" in the form of bonus checks. Such an act would violate both state and federal campaign finance laws.

Maybe Fox was right. Nothing says "dedication to the community" like giving back money in the form of illegal campaign contributions.

As a not-for-profit entity, the Fiesta Bowl itself can't make donations to politicians. State campaign finance records show that since 2000, fourteen Fiesta Bowl employees donated more than $38,000 to politicians, according to the *Republic*. Five former employees told the newspaper how the alleged scam worked. They often made donations on the same day and to the same candidates as Junker, then soon after were paid back with checks in the form of merit pay. The Arizona attorney general is investigating the matter.

The Fiesta Bowl did acknowledge to the newspaper that it spent $4 million during the same period "on lobbyists, trips, dinners, and golf retreats to build relationships with athletic officials who control the Bowl Championship Series and to garner support from politicians." That's $4 million that could and should be sitting in the coffers of colleges that need it or the bank accounts of real charities that depend on it.

Instead, it was just millions upon millions more wasted in protecting the Cartel.

4 Lies, Damn Lies, and Bowl Payouts

It was December 2008, three weeks from kickoff, and the Motor City Bowl still needed a team to play Central Michigan. When the regular season ended, seventy-one teams had been bowl-eligible by virtue of winning at least six games. Bids went out. Matchups were set. Now only five teams remained available to the Motor City Bowl and its executive director, Ken Hoffman.

Rather than court any of those teams, he waited for his phone to ring.

A flurry of calls ensued, and Hoffman checked the incoming numbers. Area code 408. It was athletic officials from San Jose State. Area code 561. Florida Atlantic wanted in. Thus commenced a bidding war, though not the traditional sort. The schools were bargaining for the right to play in the Motor City Bowl, and the winner would be whichever decided to take the least money of the game's advertised $750,000-per-team payout.

San Jose State offered to take just $250,000 and accept the rest in face-value tickets, even though those tickets would be hard to give away, much less sell, for an anonymous bowl game in iced-over Detroit.

Florida Atlantic offered to relinquish all cash and, as compensation, take $750,000 in tickets to a stadium that would have tens of thousands of empty seats. For the honor of playing in a D-list bowl, Florida Atlantic was willing to be paid nothing.

Soon, Hoffman announced the Motor City Bowl's matchup. Central Michigan's opponent would be Florida Atlantic. And the media continued to suggest a payout of $750,000 per team.

To paraphrase Mark Twain, there are three kinds of lies: lies, damned lies, and bowl payouts.

Bowl games advertise big, flashy payouts, which leave fans with the impression they're profitable and beneficial for every participating team and part of a positive system that must, at all costs, be preserved.

Sorry, but it's all a shell game, a sweetheart deal between the bowls' fat cats and the Cartel that ties universities to a backward system affecting the Granddaddy of Them All down to the Lowliest of Them All. When athletic departments compare actual payouts with expenses, the collective profits are dramatically slimmer than advertised, and the bowl system is more boondoggle than moneymaker. The majority of bowl games leave schools in the red, requiring conferences to pool bowl payouts and take revenue generated by BCS games to cover the losses from lower-tier ones, such as the Motor City Bowl.

Bowl games don't pay for transportation. Or lodging. Or most of the teams' meals. So shortly after cutting the deal with the Motor City Bowl, Florida Atlantic athletic director Craig Angelos sat in his office trying to figure out how avoid losing hundreds of thousands of dollars. He's the rare AD who doesn't get a bonus just for reaching a money-losing bowl game. He's rewarded for balancing the department budget, and he needed to figure out how to do that for a game that paid Florida Atlantic nothing.

He decided to leave behind the school's marching band and instead partner with a high school band in Detroit, resulting in a savings of $80,000. And to make the team fly home right after the game rather than spend another night in a hotel, which would've cost $10,000. And to bring in only six cheerleaders and a mascot one day before the game, which set him back only $1,090. Even with the scrimping and scratching, and with more than a quarter million dollars given to the program by the Sun Belt Conference, Florida Atlantic still needed to come up with $41,196 to cover its 126-person traveling party for the Motor City Bowl, money the nonexistent payout never reimbursed.

"The good news is you get to go to a bowl game," Angelos said. "The heavy lifting comes when you're trying to make the numbers work."

Often the numbers don't work and end up costing schools hundreds of thousands of dollars, an examination of public records shows. Going to a bowl game is no cheap affair. Bonuses for coaches and athletic department staffers, tied to bowl-game appearances, have soared. Alabama paid $1.3 million in bonuses to coaches and athletic-department officials after the 2010 BCS championship game.

On top of that, the team, athletic administration, cheerleaders, band, and university brass travel to an often-distant location for up to eight nights, as stipulated by most bowl contracts. Ohio State, for instance, spent $2 million on travel, meals, and entertainment for its appearance in the 2010 Rose Bowl.

The most onerous part of the bowl racket is the so-called ticket guarantee, which requires teams to buy thousands of full-price seats they can rarely resell in full. While athletic directors may be foolish enough to pay face value for tickets, fans aren't. Since so few games sell out, fans know to wait for prices to plummet online. On the day of the 2009 Music City Bowl, tickets were available for 19 cents on StubHub.

It all adds up to the illusion of made money—bowl payouts trumpeted loudly, costs rarely acknowledged.

In 2008, the Papajohns.com Bowl advertised a payout of $300,000 per team yet required each school to sell 10,000 tickets, which cost both athletic departments $400,000. While Rutgers beat North Carolina State 29–23, nearly half of the 71,594-seat Legion Field in Birmingham, Alabama, sat empty, and both teams were financial losers. For $300,000 and a pizza bowl appearance, N.C. State spent $730,000 and Rutgers spent almost $1.2 million.

In Rutgers' case, the school sold just 4,650 tickets, absorbing a loss of $214,000 off the bat. Qualifying for a bowl game triggered bonuses for the coaches, almost $270,000 worth of extra pay for leading the school to a game that resulted in hundreds of thousands of dollars in losses. Not that Rutgers coach Greg Schiano can be blamed for the out-of-control expenses that make these games so popular among Cartel members. Rutgers epitomized wasteful spending during its $1.2 million trip to the Papajohns.com Bowl.

Twenty-one Rutgers executives and administrators spent $28,950 getting to and from the game ($1,378.57 per person). On the ground, they blew an additional $60,168 over six days. That's an average of $478 a day on room, food, and booze, no small feat in Birmingham, Alabama.

At the time, Rutgers was coming off a New Jersey state audit into the school's spending for its trip to the 2006 Texas Bowl. The investigation found the school had violated its own expense policies. Spending was out of control, with $11,000 going to such incidentals as in-room movies and valet parking.

The University of Iowa spent $328,340 for its band to attend the 2009 Outback Bowl. It wasn't only for transportation, hotels, and meals, either. The Outback doesn't miss a beat when bilking a participating university.

The Hawkeye Marching Band provided free halftime entertainment for the game, allowing Tampa Bay Bowl Association Inc. to avoid hiring a professional act. The Orange Bowl spent $531,250 on its elaborate show in 2009, according to tax records. Rather than show its appreciation for a free show, the Outback charged Iowa $65 per game ticket for each of the 346 members of the band's traveling party. Total cost: $22,490. In bowl games, not even the band gets in free.

It's not like the Outback was hurting for the money, either. It turned a profit on the game and ended fiscal 2008 with $9.8 million in assets, including nearly $5 million in cash, according to tax records. It's no surprise considering bowls have figured out how to turn a profit on halftime. The Outback Bowl isn't the lone guilty party. The only people not charged for tickets at most bowl games are the players and coaches. For a group of entities that the Cartel is so happy to paint as "partners" with the schools, the bowls are like a shady talent agent who is utterly elated to showcase a band's talent . . . as long as the band can drop twenty grand for the privilege of working with him. What the Cartel calls a partnership is actually a fleecing.

Iowa was shorn to the skin by the Outback Bowl, which chose the school even though Northwestern had a better record (9-3 to 8-4) and defeated the Hawkeyes during the 2008 regular season. The decision was typical of bowls: The Outback opted not for the best team but the one whose fans traditionally go to bowl games in larger numbers. And everyone in the bowl business knows Iowa travels better than Northwestern. The more fans in tow, the more tickets sold, and ticket sales account for the largest portion of revenue for most bowl games.

Almost all bowl games require a ticket guarantee. The Outback Bowl's number for Iowa and South Carolina: eleven thousand apiece. In the New Year's Day game, the Hawkeyes spanked the Gamecocks 31–10. The ticket guarantee returned the favor to Iowa's athletic department, leaving it $150,000 in the hole from unsold pieces of paper.

This led to no mea culpa, of course. Administrators do not apologize. They release statements prepared for them by under-lings who specialize in the ancient language of spin. The open letter from Iowa athletic director Gary Barta was particularly rich—and even more interesting when contrasted with reality.

The letter: "History indicated demand from our fans for this particular game and destination would be strong, and it was."

The reality: Barta may be the only person in the world who would deem the demand leading to a $150,000 bath "strong."

The letter: "The consensus was that more than twenty thou-sand fans of the Hawkeyes made the trip to Tampa. Unfortu-nately, many of those fans chose to purchase their game tickets either locally or through Ticketmaster, and those don't help us in terms of (the school) getting credit for those sales."

The reality: Those ticket sales—whether handled by Tick-etmaster, StubHub, or the game's ticket office—did guarantee the Outback Bowl and its well-paid officials a handsome profit. The bowl wins. The school and its conference lose.

The letter: "Ticket sales directly through our ticket office ranked in the top 15 among sixty-four schools that participated in bowl games last winter and the top 10 of the non-BCS games. We also did quite well compared to our Big Ten peers."

The reality: While Iowa ate $150,000 in unsold tickets, other schools gorged themselves sicker. Western Michigan was re-quired to pay $450,000 for eleven thousand tickets to its 2008 Texas Bowl game against Rice, according to the *San Diego Union-Tribune*. The Broncos sold just 548 tickets, leaving them $412,535 in the hole.

Maryland had $135,000 in tickets to the 2009 Humanitarian Bowl go unsold. Furthermore, it cost the Terrapins $480,000 to fly the team and the travel party to the game in Boise, Idaho, and back. Meals and lodging cost another $210,000. Before it was over, the school had spent nearly $1 million to play in a game with a listed payout of $750,000.

The problem extends beyond mid-level teams at lower-tier bowls. Even the biggest programs at the biggest games bleed heavily. Ohio State was obligated to buy 17,500 tickets to the 2009 Fiesta Bowl, according to NCAA records. It sold 9,983, losing a cool $1 million. The Buckeyes couldn't even sell out their 2010 Rose Bowl allotment, eating $144,710 in empty seats.

Virginia Tech sold less than 20 percent of its required 17,500-ticket allotment for the 2009 Orange Bowl, according to school documents. The Hokies and the ACC combined to pay full price for 14,158 empty seats to the game. Net loss: $1.77 million. It was part of an epic bath that the Orange Bowl laid on the school. Virginia Tech's expense allowance from the ACC was $1.6 million. It wound up spending $3.8 million.

"The majority of the bowls are underwritten by the conferences to provide postseason opportunities," said Gene Bleymaier, athletic director at Boise State. "On paper you might get a payout. But you're giving it right back to them because you're required to buy tickets and/or sponsorships.

"The bowl says, 'I'm going to give you $750,000, but you're required to sell $600,000 worth of tickets and $100,000 in sponsorships,'" said Bleymaier, who also serves on the board of directors of the Humanitarian Bowl. "[Schools] do it so they can say they went to a bowl game."

Wisconsin spent $1.2 million on a trip to the Champs Sports Bowl. A bid to the Gator Bowl required that Nebraska take responsibility for 12,750 tickets for its game against Clemson. Unsold tickets and comps cost the Cornhuskers more than $120,000.

"Half to two-thirds of all bowl ticket sales are basically a money push," Mountain West commissioner Craig Thompson said. "I've got to pay for my ten thousand tickets, so here's my

OFFICIAL SUMMARY OF VIRGINIA TECH 2009 ORANGE BOWL EXPENSES

Summary of Postseason Football Institutional Bowl Expenses for 2008–09

Participating institution: Virginia Polytechnic Institute & State University
Name of bowl game: Orange Bowl
Date of bowl game: January 1, 2009

PARTICIPATING INSTITUTION'S REVENUE

Expense allowance from conference (if applicable):	$ 1,600,000

PARTICIPATING INSTITUTION'S EXPENSES

Transportation costs (please list):

Team and staff total cost:	$	183,524
Number of days traveled:		8
Number in travel party:		171
Band and cheerleaders total cost:	$	**101,607**
Number of days traveled:		7
Number in travel party:		434
Official party (faculty, athletics dept., etc.) total cost:	$	**102,964**
Number of days traveled:		8
Number in travel party:		136
Subtotal Transportation Expense:	$	**388,095**

Meals/Lodging Per Diem:

Team and staff:	$	446,283
Band and cheerleaders:	$	258,329
Official party (faculty, athletics dept., etc.):	$	66,776
SUBTOTAL MEALS/LODGING PER DIEM EXPENSE:	$	**771,388**

Entertainment:	$	40,000
Promotion:	$	11,541
Awards:	$	80,995
Equipment and supplies:	$	69,800
*Tickets (line 3.c. from below):	$	1,769,750
Administrative:	$	100,907
Other (please detail below):	$	586,428
supplemental compensation, wages, FICA		
TOTAL EXPENSES:		**$ 3,818,904**

Should include only the amount the institution and/or conference absorbed from unsold tickets.

PARTICIPATING INSTITUTION'S TICKET COMMITMENT

	Number	Ticket Price	Total
1) Tickets committed:			
a. By institution	6,750	$ 125	$ 843,750
b. By conference	10,750	$ 125	$ 1,343,750
2) Tickets sold:			
a. By institution	3,342	$ 125	$ 417,750
b. By conference	0	$ 125	$ 0
3) Tickets absorbed:			
a. By institution	3,408	$ 125	$ 426,000
b. By conference	10,750	$ 125	$ 1,343,750
c. Total of tickets absorbed:	14,158	$ 125	$ 1,769,750

check for $600,000. Then you pay me the $750,000 'bowl payout.' Why even go through the charade? Why don't I just buy the 3,800 tickets my fans want? Or don't make me buy tickets and don't pay me anything.

"They only do it for the public-relations value. It isn't a real figure. They've just inflated it and come up with this $750,000 number because it sounds good."

Sounding good matters most to bowl games. Six bowls—the Capital One, Cotton, Independence, Las Vegas, Motor City, and Humanitarian actually pay less in inflation-adjusted money today than they did in 1998. And that's just if you believe their listed payouts, which the Motor City proves aren't real.

Creative accounting helps preserve the illusion that all bowl games are profitable for schools. Most conferences pool bowl payouts, allowing a BCS bid to cover the costs for money-losing mid- and lower-tier bowls. According to official BCS payout documents, the power conferences were guaranteed at least $19.8 million in 2010. Many conferences cut each school a check whether or not it participated. Others offer extra for participating teams to defray costs. The system allows lower-tier bowl teams to live off the welfare of BCS bowl teams, yet in the grand scheme, the pooling of bowl revenue costs everyone millions.

The University of Florida's appearance in the 2009 BCS title game came with an advertised payout of $17.5 million. That may have sounded good. It's actually a case study in how the Cartel plays financial three-card monte to make the bowls look better. The SEC took the money, along with the payouts from seven other bowls in which conference teams participated. It then divided that money up thirteen ways (one for each of the league's twelve teams and one for the conference office). It also provided extra to Florida since it reached the title game, giving the Gators a total payout of $2.467 million.

Between coaches' bonuses ($960,000), travel costs ($681,000), tickets ($320,000), band and cheerleaders ($190,000), and other expenses, the total to travel across the state to Miami Gardens was $2.42 million, according to a *South Florida Sun-Sentinel* report. For winning the BCS championship game, Florida made $47,000.

"There is a perception that we make $17 million because the public sees that payout number, but the data doesn't show that," Florida spokesman Steve McClain told the *Sun-Sentinel*.

The sharing of bowl revenue to cover up losses of teams participating in smaller bowls is financial sleight of hand–turned–P.R. ploy. By having it appear that no school lost any money, no athletic directors have to explain how they blew a million dollars. It also means that some of the nation's best teams—even those that win a national championship—might not make any money on their bowl appearances.

To say no school lost money is an assault on sensibility, a line only a group of bureaucrats who've never run an actual business could claim. In the real world, any business that suffers from inefficient operations, duplicate services, and outdated contracts that drive up costs and eat into earnings doesn't sit idly and shrug its shoulders. It does everything in its power to correct the practices. Lost profits count as lost money.

No college football team, let alone one the stature of Florida, would ever play a regular-season game for $47,000. Gators home games gross an estimated $5 million. In 2009, Florida paid lowly Charleston Southern $450,000—or nearly ten times what it made on the BCS title game—to play in Gainesville. For participating in the nearest thing to a preseason bowl, the Chick-fil-A Kickoff Game in Atlanta, Alabama and Virginia Tech were each paid "at least $2.3 million" in 2009, according to the *Sports-Business Journal*.

When your team deserves at least $2.3 million and winds up with about $47,000, you lost money. Like $2.253 million of it.

Bowl directors estimate that only fourteen of the thirty-five games generate a legitimate profit for the participating teams. While the twenty-one other bowls place additional burden on the schools and conferences, they serve the BCS backers well. When the outcry for a playoff swells, the status quo squad trots out its standard reply, and it includes such tired flimflam as: A playoff could jeopardize the future of these bowl games and deny athletes the cherished bowl-game trip experience.

Sanity reared its noble head, however briefly, in 2001, when the Humanitarian Bowl courted a 7-4 UCLA team. The Bruins had started 6-0 and appeared to be a contender for the national championship before they lost three of their last four games. Despite the late-season swoon, they remained an appealing team for a mid-tier game like the Humanitarian Bowl, played on the signature blue turf in Boise.

Pete Dalis, then in his last year as UCLA's athletic director, ended the talks before Humanitarian Bowl officials made a formal offer. Then, as now, the Humanitarian Bowl advertised a payout of $750,000 per team—a claim that warrants fine print and full disclosure. Dalis, in explaining his decision, turned into a bowl-game whistle-blower. He cited the Humanitarian's requirements—such as the responsibility for selling 5,000 tickets at $33 each, a donation in the form of a "corporate sponsorship," and a minimum stay of five nights in Boise—and said that UCLA stood to lose $300,000 if it accepted a bid to a game that advertised a payout of $750,000.

"UCLA felt a fiduciary responsibility to at least break even in the bowl game," Dalis said at the time. "We never said we weren't interested in playing in the game, just unwilling to lose several hundred thousand dollars to play."

Eight years later, fiduciary responsibility remains little more than a quaint notion. Case in point: In December 2008, losing money was a secondary concern for San Jose State and Florida

Atlantic, then both 6-6 after the regular season and chiefly concerned about getting into a bowl game. Their hopes—or perhaps delusions—were that the publicity and visibility associated
with a bowl game appearance would pay off in recruiting, fundraising, and ticket sales. That December, when it cut its deal
with the Motor City Bowl, Florida Atlantic felt it needed every
possible jolt in hopes of building a new home on its Boca Raton,
Florida, campus by the 2010 season.

The school had approved the construction of a 30,000-seat
stadium and was still looking for private donations to close the
financial gap for the $62 million project. The goal: a fall 2010
opening. Until then, Florida Atlantic would play its home games
at Lockhart Stadium, an 18,500-seat stadium fifteen miles from
campus and light years from the elite facilities of big-time college football. Florida Atlantic desperately wanted to be big-time,
so it scraped the money together, did its belt-tightening best to
make its way to Detroit, and walked out onto the field for the
Motor City Bowl a proud team.

With their cheerleaders and mascot arriving at the last minute, with their high school band in place, with their travel party
thinned like a wrestler trying to shave off those last few ounces,
the Florida Atlantic Owls took the field and delivered an upset
with a 24–21 victory over Central Michigan. Soon enough, the
Owls would begin to evaluate the early returns on their bowl-
trip investment.

On National Signing Day two months after the victory, Florida Atlantic signed twenty-six recruits, and Rivals.com ranked
the class eighty-ninth among Division I-A teams. None of the
twenty-six players who signed with the Owls lived anywhere
near Detroit. All but one hailed from Florida. At least they
were eighty-ninth. It was better than Florida Atlantic's classes
of 2008 (101st) and 2007 (118th).

It didn't last. On signing day in 2010, Florida Atlantic hauled in the 120th-ranked class in the country, according to Rivals .com. Its batch of recruits was the worst of the seven biggest programs in Florida. It was the worst, too, in the nine-team Sun Belt, generally regarded as the weakest conference in major college football. Florida Atlantic's class, in fact, was rated the lowest in all of Division I-A football: 120th of 120 teams.

The newest recruits won't get to see the new stadium until at least their sophomore year. In August 2009, citing the economic downturn, Florida Atlantic announced the scheduled opening had been delayed by a year. Michigan State canceled its trip to Boca Raton in 2010. The contract specified the Spartans would meet the Owls in the new stadium. Big Ten teams, and big-time teams, don't do tiny stadiums.

Big-time teams don't lose multiple games in the worst conference in America, either. In 2009, Florida Atlantic finished 5-7 and failed to qualify for a bowl game. There was no sign of a return on investment from the Motor City Bowl excursion. And anyone who thinks dividends will be realized in time should take heed of what Dalis told *USA Today* after he adhered to the bottom line and refused to lose money on a trip to the Humanitarian Bowl.

"I think a lot of schools feel very strongly that, no matter what the cost, they have to go to a bowl game," he said. "In my nineteen years in this business, I've found they really don't alter the future. I think it's a myth."

Mark Twain would have been less polite. He would have called the advertised bowl payouts what they really are.

A lie.

5 High-Paid Blazers

The bowl system is ripe for financial abuse. Despite enjoying nonprofit status, there is plenty of profit. Much of it, in fact, ends up back in people's pockets. The same people who aid and abet the Cartel in its defiling of college football. There is no other way to explain how bowl executives haul in outrageous salaries when their entire year revolves around preparing for one game. Some schools stage as many as eight home games a season, and they certainly don't pay their operations directors half a million dollars.

And yet that's nearly how much Rick Baker, the executive director of the Cotton Bowl, received in compensation for 2007, according to tax records. Baker made $490,433, and that doesn't include fringe benefits, transportation, travel, and a healthy expense account. He's not the only one getting fat on bowls, either. Nearly two dozen bowl directors earned more than $300,000 in total compensation, according to federal tax filings. Sugar Bowl CEO Paul Hoolahan pocketed $607,500. John Junker of the Fiesta and Insight Bowls received a total of $457,356. Alamo Bowl CEO Derrick Fox took in $438,044. The Chick-fil-A Bowl in Atlanta sent $931,608 for "primarily salaries" to the local chamber of commerce that oversees the game.

"Why does the executive director of the Cotton Bowl get almost a half a million dollars a year to stage a one-week series

of events that culminate in an exhibition football game?" Rep.
Joe Barton (R-Texas) said. "I would've thought they had volunteers who do most of that, and they paid the executive director
$60,000 or $75,000 to answer the mail and attend chamber
events."

Barton is not one to complain about salaries. Rank-and-file
members of the United States House of Representatives enjoy an
annual salary of $174,000, which puts them in the top 10 per-
cent of all earners in America. He repeatedly acknowledges how
lucky he is. He simply can't fathom what constitutes an income
near $500,000 for running a football game when the participat-
ing teams pay their own travel expenses and sell their own
tickets, and an army of unpaid workers do the executive director's bidding. Neither, it seems, could Baker. He took a pay cut
in 2008 and made only $356,154 to manage the same one game.

It's not like Baker is some entrepreneur who started the
thing. The Cotton Bowl is in its seventh-fourth year, and if
seven decades have proven anything, it's that bowl games might
as well be licenses to mine gold. While fledgling games regularly used to go out of business (Seattle Bowl, Cherry Bowl),
the revenue that filters toward bowls today makes them almost
fail-safe.

"Maybe I should switch jobs and run one of these bowls,"
Barton said, and he's got a point: In the United States, home of
the get-rich-quick scheme, running a bowl may be the cushiest
gig of all. Bowls expanded rapidly for a reason, and with thirty-
five this year and an expected thirty-eight in the 2011 season,
it's not slowing down. As long as bowls make decisions with
money in mind, someone new will want to join the gravy train.

The salaries are extraordinary, and it doesn't take a major
bowl to rake in money. The Emerald Bowl, a lower-tier game in
San Francisco since renamed the Kraft Fight Hunger Bowl, was

thrifty by bowl standards in fiscal 2008, totaling $2.9 million in expenditures. About 10.8 percent of the game's revenue went to executive director Gary Cavalli, and the $320,492 in salary did not include benefits or other accoutrements.

Just how out of control bowl executive director salaries are cannot be answered simply, as there are few comparable jobs in the world of not-for-profit organizations. Bowl executives often make more than their local college athletic director, a position with far greater demands and responsibilities. The executive director of the New Orleans Area Habitat for Humanity, who spearheaded construction for people displaced by Hurricane Katrina, was paid $95,000 in fiscal 2007, according to tax records—about 15 percent of what the Sugar Bowl director got.

Of course, running a bowl isn't simple. It is, in many cases, very simple. It's not far-fetched to suggest just about anyone with minimal game-management experience could sell out the Georgia Dome for a New Year's Eve game between a local school (Georgia Tech) and the defending national champion (Louisiana State). That was the 2008 Chick-fil-A Bowl: a true open-the-doors, print-the-tickets, and count-the-cash night.

How the Chick-fil-A operates takes neither a quantum physicist nor a pathologist to understand. Its M.O. is simple enough for a business-school dropout: exploit a cushy date and time (New Year's Eve) and broadcast partner (ESPN), and invite two nearby teams that will sell reams of tickets. The low-hanging fruit is sweetest to the Chick-fil-A Bowl, on-field competitiveness be damned. All the hullabaloo from the Cartel about how the regular season means everything and needs to be guarded at all costs simply isn't important to bowl directors, who favor proximity and passion more than actual results.

This is the system the Cartel fights for: one in which most bowl executives, clad in their garish blazers, personally pocket hundreds of thousands of dollars while turning college football's postseason into a revenue-grabbing free-for-all. You can fault the bowl directors only so much. They are businessmen getting what they can from a bureaucracy that invites them to pilfer. They've found a willing partner, in part because increasingly the athletic director who is supposed to guard his school's money gets a cut of the action, too.

Reaching a bowl game isn't difficult for any team, and it's particularly easy for a school from one of the big six conferences. During the 2009–10 bowl season, forty-five of the sixty-five teams from those leagues (almost 70 percent) went to a game. Many of the appearances were money losers that require schools to use conference revenue sharing to cover the loss.

"The fact we didn't go to a bowl game the last two years means we actually made money," said former Michigan AD Bill Martin, trying to find the only bright side of the Wolverines' recent struggles.

In most businesses, blowing the company's resources is cause for dismissal. Athletic directors have convinced their presidents that this isn't just a positive. It's cause for a sizeable merit bonus.

Nowhere else could employees trick their bosses into thinking that avoiding the bottom 30 percent of their professional peer group warrants a five-figure pop. And yet Missouri athletic director Mike Alden receives an extra month's pay ($23,947.92) if the Tigers go to even the lowliest bowl game. Arizona State's Lisa Love picks up a $13,115.38 bonus for any bowl appearance by the Sun Devils. North Carolina's Dick Baddour earns $24,583.33. For years, West Virginia's Ed Pastilong received $30,000. These are just a few examples among many; any AD that doesn't get big money for a small bowl needs a new agent.

For agreeing to that lopsided 2009 Fiesta Bowl deal—in which Ohio State spent $1.7 million in travel and entertainment costs, wasted $1 million on empty seats, and went $820,000 over the Big Ten's expense allowance, according to university records— Buckeyes athletic director Gene Smith picked up a $54,000 bonus. It was hardly a harmless, easily recovered, cost-of-doing-business expenditure. Smith soon thereafter announced he was raising football and men's basketball ticket prices, plus fees at the school golf course, to help offset a projected revenue shortfall. John Junker's Fiesta Bowl, flush with the Buckeyes' money, had no such budgetary concerns.

Even some assistant ADs and other mid-level staffers are in on the deal. At Virginia Tech, the director and assistant director of the school band get $4,000 and $2,000, respectively, for any bowl trip. Sure, it might make financial sense for the school to decline a sure loser of a bowl invite, but then none of the bosses would get their year-end bump.

Let's be clear on the scam that's going on here: Lower-tier bowls exist solely because athletic directors are willing to lose their employers' money to prop the games up. There is no bowl game without the university's open checkbook to buy tickets they won't sell and support other expenses. Yet the ADs have persuaded their employers to handsomely reward them for going to an event that wouldn't exist without the school.

It's little wonder so many ADs support the status quo, argue to protect the current system, and gleefully blow big money so games can remain in business. Or that almost no AD ever turns down a bowl invite, preferring to wax on about the intangible benefits of the appearance. It's even less surprising that the number of bowl games keeps growing, or that the Big 12 pushed through a rule change that allows bowl games to select a 6-6 team from a power conference ahead of a team with a superior record from another league. There's even talk of petitioning the NCAA to deem 5-7 teams bowl eligible.

Critics contend that the proliferation of bowl games is college football's version of participation trophies. Everyone's a winner. The Cartel cackles at such innocence. Forget the trophy, just cut the check.

Understanding the compromised position of the athletic director on the other side of the bargaining table, bowl directors are so comfortable with their place they don't bother denying their motivation is straight profit.

Ken Hoffman was the sports information director at Michigan State until 1997, when he teamed with former Spartans coach George Perles and created the Motor City Bowl in metro Detroit. With its slot in the bowl calendar a day or two after Christmas, it became an immediate punch line. Who, exactly, wanted to spend Christmas in Detroit?

Fans of the Mid-American Conference living in Michigan or Ohio, it turned out, had no problem with the Motor City Bowl. After a few years of tinkering, Hoffman found the proper formula for profit, matching a MAC team against a national program desperate for any bowl scraps. Occasionally, he even drew a Big Ten team.

The game draws about 40,000-plus fans annually and enjoys an ESPN deal. When the American auto industry collapsed, killing sponsorship from Detroit's automakers, Hoffman got local pizza magnate Mike Ilitch to come aboard and rebrand the game the Little Caesar's Pizza Bowl. Even in a city beset by unemployment and desolation, a bowl of minor import didn't just survive. It thrived.

Hoffman doesn't hide behind his motivation: He wants to sell tickets. It's why he focuses on local teams. He'll happily take two MAC teams if they'll draw a crowd. And any mediocre team from the state of Michigan might as well book its trip to Detroit. In 2008, Hoffman had a choice of the MAC's actual champion, Buffalo, or a 12-1 Ball State team that spent most of the season in the national polls and was on the cusp of cracking the BCS before losing the conference championship. Instead, the bowl invited a Central Michigan team that wound up losing three straight games to end the season. It was the only school with a big enough alumni base in Detroit to assure ticket sales.

Though the game still draws snickers, Hoffman took it private at the turn of the century and has since expanded his company. He ran the International Bowl in Toronto for three years and said he would start another game if he could secure the proper conference tie-ins. Forget size. Even the smallest bowl game can be a hugely profitable venture.

The system ensures so. Not only do schools support bowl games with crazy ticket guarantees, they treat the bowl representatives like royalty. Consider the infamous bowl scouts, relics from a bygone era that persist today despite their patent uselessness. In the 1970s, when few regular-season games were televised and bowls actually tried to piece together attractive matchups—not just schools that would agree to tickets in lieu of payout—they would send talent evaluators to figure out whether a team was a worthwhile candidate.

Since there were only about a dozen bowl games, the selection committees could be choosy. Schools responded by wining and dining the scout in an effort to win goodwill and garner a coveted bid. Bowl scouts were lavished with prime hotel rooms in town, the best parking spots at the stadium, and tickets with press box and sideline access. The school president might throw a private cocktail party for them. Bowl scouts mattered, even if their mission and skills were dubious.

Little, in that respect, has changed. Every week, a herd of

bowl scouts—these days often cronies of the game's executive director—scatters across the country living a fan's dream life. Scouts can see Oklahoma-Texas one week and Notre Dame–USC another, and it's all for free—or, at least, at the expense of the bowl game and university.

"I call them the March of the Entitled," said a major college assistant athletic director, who for years has spent Friday nights throwing parties for bowl scouts. "They show up and want their ass kissed, steak and scotch. Every single weekend we have to entertain these guys, and they aren't even scouting, they're just here for a good time. I've been arguing for years we stop, but no one will."

Often the scouting trips are wildly impractical or thinly veiled attempts to score free tickets to the game of the week. The Chick-fil-A, for instance, scouts as many as nine games a weekend, often sending two people, even though a DirecTV hook-up and a roomful of flat-screen TVs could offer the same perspective at a fraction of the price.

For its 2007 game, the Sugar Bowl spent $272,231 on its selection committee, even though, as a BCS game, its choice was obvious. The Sugar Bowl picked LSU against Notre Dame, snagging the local team for ticket sales and the nation's biggest TV draw for a deeper impact. Not a single scout needed to see a single snap all season for Sugar Bowl brass to pair the Tigers and the Irish.

In 2009, when No. 3 Alabama hosted No. 9 LSU, a rep from the lowly Papajohns.com Bowl showed up at Bryant-Denny Stadium. Either a bowl game that wound up with two unranked 7-5 teams actually considered the possibility of landing a top 10 SEC powerhouse, or somebody was jonesing for a trip to Tuscaloosa. If, by some accident of nature, Alabama was available, no bowl scout was needed to inform the blazers that the Crimson Tide was indeed worthy of a pizza bowl berth.

And you wonder why bowl executives stand in front of Congress and spit misinformation under oath to elected officials. They've got the golden goose that drank from the Fountain of Youth. They're paid hundreds of thousands of dollars to go on fourteen football party weekends with their friends.

With a playoff, perhaps the lifestyle gets reined in and bowls learn a thing or two about financial pragmatism. The ones who suffer the most: the Cartel's leeching bowl executives, who will learn quickly that they can't suck their games dry without consequences. If other fat goes, suddenly the half-million-dollar salaries could be scrutinized.

Imagine the Kraft Fight Hunger Bowl—the little game that could, with its title sponsor vowing to help solve one of the nation's most endemic issues—assessing Gary Cavalli's salary and wondering how one person really deserves nearly 11 percent of the company's revenue. It's plenty more equitable to halve that, in which case Cavalli would make $160,246 a year to run a semi-anonymous football game that takes place once a year.

In other words, he'd be paid like a mere United States congressman.

6 Presidential Problem

Harvey Perlman is the chancellor of the University of Nebraska-Lincoln. He's a learned man, an accomplished lawyer who spends his days trying to figure out how to run an institution that earns prestigious Carnegie Research status. He also serves as the chair of the BCS Presidential Oversight Committee, a job perfect for someone like Perlman. In exchange for playing puppet to the Cartel and repeating its intellectually bankrupt drivel, Perlman gets a fancy title that appeals to the gridiron-mad Cornhusker State.

Perlman does not understand football, of course. He can't. Because no Nebraska-born, Nebraska-raised, Nebraska-educated, and, for more than three decades, Nebraska-employed person would do what Perlman did: laugh at the viability of a playoff with on-campus games. In rejecting the possibility of postseason football at legendary venues such as Nebraska's Memorial Stadium, Perlman gives the impression that, well, Nebraska stinks.

"You're . . . going to have to play at home sites—which I'm sure everybody will want to play in Nebraska in December and January," he told the *Nebraska State Paper* with a heavy sheen of sarcasm. Which was met by an equal dose of scorn, since the truth is, yeah, the prospect of a game in Nebraska in December and January *does* thrill just about everybody.

Nebraska fans, for example, wouldn't oppose watching their

Cornhuskers in some of the most important games ever staged in the legendary stadium. Better that than traveling to some dull municipal facility for a bowl game in an unfamiliar place that doesn't carry the smell of Runza meat pies and Big Red hot dogs, staples of Nebraska home games.

And surely the out-of-town fans and television viewers would love seeing the blizzard of red that fills the famed 81,067-seat stadium. The Heisman and Outland trophy displays, the statue of Tom Osborne, the Blackshirt defense—college football enthusiasts appreciate history and tradition, and Nebraska teems with as much as any school.

Nebraska players and coaches would cherish the chance, too. Games in front of a partisan crowd filled with friends and family. The opportunity to finally see how those SEC teams handle an icy field and bone-chilling winds. The prospect of riding home-field advantage, the reward for a superlative regular season, to a national championship.

Most of all, the people to whom Perlman should answer, his students and faculty, reap the benefits. In a time of budget cuts and soaring tuition, Nebraska—and every college and university in the country, for that matter—could use the millions of dollars a playoff would send its way.

And better yet, it would pour millions back into the city of Lincoln. If regular-season games are a boon, imagine the playoffs, with increased out-of-town media, higher ticket prices, and an even more hyped atmosphere. Hotels, restaurants, bars, grocery stores, parking garages, and the university would all swim in cash. Apparently, Perlman is more interested in filling the coffers of some town in Florida or Texas with Nebraskans' money.

"We would love a [playoff] game here," said Wendy Birdsall, president of the Lincoln Chamber of Commerce. "I'm an economic developer. I'm all for looking for opportunities for the community and bringing in revenue."

What, then, is Perlman's rationale to scoff at his university's destination stadium, his community's need for economic stimulus, and the chance to market Nebraska's flagship campus? Certainly it can't be the weather, as Perlman subtly alludes. You can't argue against snowflakes, which have kissed some of football's greatest games. All weather is football weather, and only a suit drunk on talking points would try to rationalize otherwise. The best game-day experience in the NFL is at Lambeau Field in Green Bay, Wisconsin, a town smaller and colder than Lincoln. It hosted perhaps the most famous football game in history, the 1967 Ice Bowl between the Green Bay Packers and Dallas Cowboys, in which the game-time wind chill was 48 degrees below zero.

Perlman makes the same mistake as all the other university presidents who align themselves with an economically underperforming system that robs fans and players: Rather than look into the BCS himself, Perlman bases his opinion almost exclusively on the very people who profit from it. "The presidents rely on being briefed principally by the conference commissioners," said Bill Martin, Michigan's retired athletic director.

It's easy to explain. Perlman has a busy university to run. So presidents ask their conference commissioners and listen to the bowl representatives that wine and dine them every December and, armed with the party line, they fight blindly.

Perlman trusted the Cartel and became a stooge for the system. A well-hewn anti-playoff excuse is that "the presidents" are against a playoff. Well, no one in the Cartel presents them with a viable playoff option. Perlman, whose career as a lawyer was rooted in the logic of an argument, otherwise would not believe that Lincoln is unworthy of hosting a football game. The

Cartel does not dare educate the educators. Finding naive university leaders such as Perlman to serve as spokesmen is one of its most brilliant ideas.

"The ones who get involved aren't reformers," said Andrew Zimbalist, a sports economist and expert on college athletics. "They're jock sniffers. They're passionate about their sports and have fun. They're not going to push for any major change. They're representing conferences, and the conferences wouldn't let them sit there if they thought they were going to change the system."

As the attacks on the BCS intensified from the halls of Congress to online chat rooms and every imaginable forum for public ridicule, the Cartel realized it needed more people to take the blame. Preferably some with more clout. So in 2003, the men who hold college football hostage turned to the men in the ivory towers and formed the Presidential Oversight Committee.

The 120 school presidents and chancellors offered authority, credentials, and brainpower. They were, in theory, academics who would ensure that athletic departments served their schools and not the other way around. Turns out they were pawns, happy to swallow the Cartel's talking points and regurgitate them.

Predictably, they cited missed classes as one of the key reasons a playoff wouldn't work. Never mind that the three lower divisions of college football run playoffs in the middle of finals and still post graduation rates higher than Division I-A. Major-conference presidents were polled for a thesis last year by James Madison University graduate student Thomas Deary, and among their top three oppositions to a playoff was the concern that "student-athletes would miss additional classes." Perlman was one of the presidents who voted that way. In a statement read before a Senate Judiciary subcommittee on antitrust issues,

Perlman further expressed concerns about a playoff "interfering with the academic calendar or impinging on the academic missions of our universities."

Perlman and his fellow presidents gleefully cash checks from college basketball, which requires exponentially more missed class time. And they relentlessly expand their conferences, with travel increasing likewise—in Nebraska's case, joining the one-thousand-mile-wide Big Ten in 2011. And at the University of Alabama, they closed the entire school for three days due to the 2010 BCS title game. Yes, the entire school.

Perlman clearly didn't think about the issue before taking a position. Organizers could conduct an entire sixteen-team playoff in the current time span it takes to put on thirty-five bowl games. Most, if not all, games would take place during semester break. The missed-class-time argument is so specious—"That's just crap," Mountain West commissioner Craig Thompson said—even the Cartel can't stand by it.

"The academic effect, it's just not a credible argument," Big Ten commissioner Jim Delany said. "I think some of the arguments that have been advanced against the playoffs have not been credible."

The Cartel would know. It authors most of them. And because its members so excel at being a moving target, no one person or group is ever responsible for the failures of the BCS. It's the presidents. The bowls. The athletic directors. The computers. The voters. The Cartel always dreams up another scapegoat. If it can cast blame toward another part of its group, the standard is safe. It's Bureaucracy Survival 101. For years, four conference commissioners passed around the role of BCS coordinator in order to share the slings and arrows tossed by the public. In 2009, they got sick of it and hired a public relations man, Bill Hancock, to do it for them. They gave him the powerful-sounding title of executive director, a position as hollow as a chocolate Easter bunny.

While Hancock ably took the mantle as public dartboard, it doesn't keep Perlman from giving the old college try. If he happens to trash his own state and argue against his university's best interests, so be it. The Cartel intended nothing less.

The more people who oppose the idea of on-campus playoff games, the better for the Cartel. It allows the perpetuation of another red herring: that a playoff would have to include bowl games as hosts. It's a key argument to making a playoff seem unworkable, because there is little doubt that trying to stage a four-week, neutral-site tournament would cause prohibitive travel costs and, consequently, half-empty stadiums.

Here's the thing: It's an argument built around a false premise—the assumption that a playoff-bowl marriage is the best option, which it decidedly isn't. A playoff doesn't have to use bowl games as neutral sites. Play the first three rounds on campus and let the bowls operate on their own outside the system.

By using campus sites until the playoff championship game, every stadium would sell out. Home fans would gobble up any unused tickets by the visiting team, and the revenues would grow exponentially. The NCAA's lower divisions and NFL each use home sites in their playoffs. The Cartel ignores this and laughably argues that Division I-AA and II and III games don't sell out. Hancock even cited the mediocre home playoff crowds at the University of Montana as an example, as though it's in any way similar to the sport's highest level. USC visiting Alabama would cause Bryant-Denny Stadium to sell out before the opening guitar riff of "Sweet Home Alabama" was complete. And that's just one of a hundred tremendous games a playoff could provide.

In its manipulation of the presidents, the Cartel has taken Lenin's old edict—a lie told often enough becomes the truth—to a new level. A lie told often enough by a Ph.D. sounds even more truthful. There's a reason so many proposed playoffs by fans and media still include using the bowl sites.

Not even the Cartel can come up with an argument for the antiseptic stadiums used at most bowls over the dozens of historic stadiums with stirring game-day environments. In their place, the Cartel offers a menagerie of dull, money-draining spots that, outside of the Rose Bowl, Sun Bowl, and a few other select stadiums, can't compete with any big-time college experience. The Citrus Bowl's grass surface was so poor for two 2009–10 bowl games that *Orlando Sentinel* columnist Mike Bianchi decried "the deplorable state of our garbage dump football stadium and the cesspool we call a playing field." No one ever wrote that about Memorial Stadium.

Leaders of self-respecting sports organizations laugh at how the bowl system works. Imagine telling NFL commissioner Roger Goodell he should take a second look at the 2010 AFC Championship game. It was played in Indianapolis, where Colts fans assured a sold-out, multimillion-dollar gate. The Colts owned the state-of-the-art building, pocketed the parking and concession money, and allowed the league to control all sponsorship rights and television revenue.

Anyone who suggested moving the game to the Citrus Bowl, where a promoter in Orlando gets up to 60 percent of the money the game generates, plus putting the NFL on the hook for all travel costs, would get thrown out of Goodell's Manhattan office. Not only does the Cartel consider this a positive arrangement, it regards the fleecing as a tradition.

Yet the system keeps the Cartel relevant, and it in turn sends its minions to preach the virtues of the BCS. If Perlman bothered to listen to his coconspirators, perhaps he would understand that in backing them he takes money out of his hometown's pocket.

During his 2009 testimony in front of Congress, Alamo Bowl CEO Derrick Fox equated playoff proponents to zealots who would rob cities of the money generated by bowl games. "They neither know nor care about the fact that those billions— yes, billions—of dollars of economic impact are generated by the existing system," Fox said.

Fox, on the other hand, neither knows nor cares that those billions—yes, billions—have "zero . . . impact" on the American economy. It's true. Just read the 2007 Valero Alamo Bowl Economic & Fiscal Impact Analysis, the very study Fox commissioned and quoted to come up with his billion-dollar figure. Fox tried to use the report, which detailed spending by out-of-town fans at San Antonio area hotels and restaurants, as the foundation for his argument. Beyond Fox's cherry-picking, the study actually ended up proving moot the Cartel's entire theory on economic impact.

When on Capitol Hill, Fox failed to mention a concept in the report called "displaced spending," which declares local fans are far less valuable to bowl cities than tourists because they would have spent their entertainment dollar elsewhere in the city.

There's no doubt about the value of out-of-town fans to local businesses. They bring money earned outside the city into it, enriching the overall economy. Local fans are different. While some San Antonians drop $100 going to the Alamo Bowl, they provide no economic impact because if there were no Alamo Bowl, they would've spent the $100 on some other business in San Antonio— a restaurant across town or at the mall on a major purchase. The money spent on the game is money not spent elsewhere.

"Most spending by local residents is considered to be displaced spending and is not counted as part of economic impact," the Alamo Bowl study said. "[The local fan] is, therefore, providing zero economic impact."

The true economic impact of bowl games depends on the size of the economy being studied. The Alamo Bowl can brag to the mayor of San Antonio about the money out-of-town visitors contribute to the local economy. If the majority of the tourists came from, say, Houston, Fox wouldn't dare be so effusive with the governor of Texas, to whom money spent in San Antonio is the same as money spent in Houston. A $100 net gain for San Antonio is a $100 net loss for Houston and zero sum for the state of Texas.

Accordingly, the Cartel's own study discredits the displaced-spending argument Fox proffered in front of Congress. By citing the revenue of all bowls, he groups them together nationally. On that scale, all spending is displaced spending, all Americans locals. Thus, the billion dollars cited in the study is, according to its own displaced-spending theory, "providing zero economic impact"—and one of the Cartel's key claims is worthless on a national scale. Leave it to the Cartel to destroy its own argument.

Using the 2010 Alamo Bowl as an example, there is no value for the American economy in taking money from Michigan State fans and putting it in Texas. Having Michigan State fans eat at a San Antonio Applebee's is no different than having them eat at an East Lansing Applebee's—except for San Antonio and East Lansing. If the Cartel wants to cite the billion dollars of economic impact for some communities, it must mention the billion dollars sucked out of the economies in other communities. And to really get technical, bowl games likely had a negative impact on the American economy. For three years, the International

Bowl was played in Toronto, and with few, if any, tourists coming from other countries to watch a game, bowls, as a whole, may have taken money out of the United States.

Even on the local level, economic impact is an increasingly dubious concept. Bowl executives now prefer to invite teams with local fan bases to the game. The last two seasons, North Carolina went to the Meineke Car Care Bowl in Charlotte. Hawaii played in the Hawaii Bowl in 2008. The Humanitarian Bowl in Boise selected Idaho in 2009. The local fans deemed less valuable by the Cartel actually anchor ticket sales and stabilize bowl revenue, economic impact be damned. Bowl executives have prioritized their own revenue from ticket sales over what communities gain from tourists.

For the 2008–09 bowl season, more than a third of the games featured a local school. Eight were from the host city or a short drive from it, and four others came from within a three-hour drive. In 2009–10, nine bowl games fell into those categories. While the University of Kentucky's Lexington campus is a three-hour, fifteen-minute drive from Nashville, where the Wildcats played in the Music City Bowl, the Kentucky state line is less than forty-five minutes away. Most Kentucky fans didn't fill Nashville hotel rooms for a week. They drove in the afternoon of the game and fled right after.

The previous season, the Music City Bowl showed even less concern for Nashville's economic impact by inviting Vanderbilt, whose campus is three miles from the game's home, LP Field. The Motor City Bowl didn't select Central Michigan three consecutive years to produce a renaissance for Detroit. Southeastern Michigan is home to the Chippewas' largest alumni base and current students who were home for Christmas. The Las Vegas Bowl has chosen Brigham Young five consecutive years because Cougars fans travel in large numbers from nearby Utah and buy tickets. It's certainly not to provide a boon for the Strip, with the majority of Mormon fans teetotaling non-gamblers.

"I think bowls' business models have changed," said Gary Stokan, president of the Chick-fil-A Bowl, which in 2009 invited Georgia Tech, situated just over a mile from the Georgia Dome. "When we all originally started, bowls were created to really develop economic impact. That's still our goal. But with the contracted payouts you have now, you've got to weigh that, balance the economic-impact figure with attendance."

Which means the local economic impact about which Fox boasted to Congress—"supporting pre- and post-Christmas business in hotels, restaurants and visitor attractions," he said—is not just nationally nonexistent. Plenty of bowls don't even care about it.

Even after Delany dismissed the academic reasoning and Stokan brought proper perspective to economic-impact fabrication, Perlman repeated the BCS boilerplate at the subcommittee hearing on July 7, 2009. He mentioned academics. He mentioned the financial impact for bowl communities. He mentioned the impossibility of staging a playoff at bowl locations. He went down the dirty laundry list of excuses.

And no one stopped or corrected Perlman, leaving him open to even more criticism. The Cartel would let him take the flak. It knows a good, naive spokesman when it sees one.

7 Myth of the Dead Bowls

Fear-mongering is an area of particular expertise for the Cartel. When comparing a playoff with the BCS, it loses the debate over excitement, fairness, and profit, so like a desperate politician interested in shifting the focus of a campaign, it goes negative. And in doing so, the Cartel tells perhaps its biggest lie of all: With a playoff system, bowl games would vanish.

"We believe the bowl system wouldn't survive a playoff," BCS executive director Bill Hancock said.

"The bowl season is dead," Big Ten commissioner Jim Delany warned in *USA Today*. "Dead."

Dead? Like, an entire month of games, vamoose, sayonara, kaput? Plenty of fans wouldn't care if a half dozen of the smaller games did expire. That's not us. If two teams want to play a college football game, we're all for it.

The demise of the Rose Bowl or the Sugar Bowl, on the other hand, is a doomsday scenario, one on which the Cartel preys. Few want to see something so beloved disappear. Others just want the chance for their favorite teams to play another game. And the Cartel thusly plays off fans' emotions.

A thorough analysis of the industry shows that the dead bowl theory is simply another Cartel myth. Bowls would continue to operate in the shadow of a playoff. Undoubtedly. The good times and good games can roll on, only without holding the sport hostage by blocking the creation of the playoff. If the question is playoff or bowls, the answer is both. The proof is in the way bowls operate fiscally and the real monetary impact of a playoff on college athletics. We studied the available financial statements, tax filings, and business plans of not-for-profit bowl games and spoke with numerous bowl executives, television deal makers, athletic directors, and conference commissioners to move past the hysteria planted by the Cartel.

The conclusion: If you love bowl games (as we do) and want to see them played for decades to come (as we do), you wouldn't oppose a playoff. You would fight for it.

The Cartel claims that all types of bowls would be wiped out—the major BCS games, the mid-tier ones, and, of course, the fledgling small events. Actually, none would.

Take the absurd implication that the Rose Bowl couldn't survive a playoff. With the game's brand, rich history, and coveted late-afternoon New Year's Day television spot—none of which would go away with a playoff—the best lawyer in the world couldn't make a case against it thriving. The game wouldn't get two conference champions, but it would still feature two major schools with huge fan bases thrilled to attend the most storied game in college football. For the January 1, 2010, game, that could've meant Penn State–Oregon State rather than Ohio State–Oregon.

The Rose Bowl's $30 million-a-year TV contract may dip in value, but television executives said it would remain at least a $15 million to $20 million property on top of selling a hundred thousand tickets and raking in parking, title sponsorship, advertising, and concessions. Right now, it's a $51 million-a-year event, according to federal tax records, and the man who for the last decade ran the Rose Bowl acknowledged a playoff would do little to the game's fortunes.

"The Rose Bowl would survive," said Mitch Dorger, the game's CEO emeritus.

Take, then, the less-prestigious, not-nearly-as-rich Chick-fil-A Bowl. Once known as the Peach Bowl, it never had anything to do with crowning a national champion and regularly invites five-loss teams. It doesn't apologize for being anything more than a fun football game.

Played New Year's Eve in Atlanta, it matches up one team from the ACC and one from the SEC, each usually within driving distance. It's a foolproof business plan, selling two big southern fan bases on the idea of watching some football and partying in Buckhead. Not only does the game routinely sell out, two of the last four years it set Georgia Dome attendance records, beating the Atlanta Falcons and the SEC title game. Facing little live sports competition, the game produced some the highest-rated bowl telecasts in ESPN history.

A playoff changes none of that. Even if the playoff plucks the best teams and forces bowls to dig deeper into the pool of eligible schools, the Chick-fil-A won't run out of 7-5 teams. If it wasn't 7-5 Tennessee in 2009, it would have been 7-5 Georgia or 7-5 South Carolina.

As is the case for most games, four main revenue streams sustain the Chick-fil-A Bowl: ticket sales, a television contract, advertising/sponsorship, and a catchall that includes fundraising, merchandise, and government aid. For its game on New Year's Eve 2008, the Chick-fil-A pitted Clemson against Auburn. It produced $12.3 million in revenue.

Tickets raised $4.3 million and sponsorship $2.6 million. ESPN paid $2.5 million to broadcast the game, and the fundraising and merchandising arm brought $2.3 million. Unlike many games, the Chick-fil-A Bowl received no direct public money. The rest of the money came mostly from interest on investments and assets.

Assuming there was a playoff, the ticket sales wouldn't change. ESPN wouldn't drop a ratings winner. Fundraising, a local endeavor, would stay the same. Even the possibility of sponsorship money drying up, which is debatable, wouldn't threaten the game's existence.

Delany asserts a playoff would suck money away from bowl games. "It's a migratory dollar," he said. "And the dollar tends to follow those areas of those elements of a competitive season that are most attractive."

Never mind the incongruity of Delany admitting a playoff is more attractive than bowl games. The migratory dollar may not be so nomadic. Sports economist Andrew Zimbalist argues that as bigger corporate sponsors drive up prices on what would be higher-rated playoff games, other companies will simply seek more-affordable options. Today, Roady's Truck Stops sponsors the Humanitarian Bowl, not the Fiesta Bowl, for a reason.

"As prices for sponsoring a playoff . . . rise, some corporations will return to the non-BCS bowls until the cost per thousand viewers (or some other metric) equalizes," Zimbalist wrote in his paper *The BCS, Antitrust and Public Policy*. ". . . The proper output metric is not the number of games, but the number of fans consuming these games and the quantity of money spent in this consumption. There are very good reasons to believe that total bowl consumption and spending will increase under a playoff system."

More specifically to the Chick-fil-A, Zimbalist said in an interview that as with any bowl game, as long as television ratings are good, sponsors will follow. "There's not going to be any problem whatsoever," he said.

For the sake of this argument, we'll go with Delany's pessimistic prediction that the sponsorship money will go to the new, shiny, and infinitely more popular kid on the block and never come back. That means $2.6 million, presumably the majority from Chick-fil-A, is at risk.

Worst-case scenario: The bowl retains 20 percent of its sponsorship, or about $500,000. Minor bowls such as the Liberty ($1.3 million) and Music City ($900,000) do better than that currently. Surely a sold-out, highly rated game will find enough local car dealers to churn up $500,000.

In that case, the Chick-fil-A would still produce $10.2 million in revenue. The bowl paid a combined $5.9 million to Auburn and Clemson in 2008. That leaves $4.3 million to stage a single football game. Since participating teams would continue to pay their own travel expenses and other costs, it leaves the true basics: Georgia Dome rent, paying referees, and other overhead. Such costs total about $1 million, according to bowl records.

That leaves $3.3 million for everything else: salaries, parties, travel for "scouting" weekends—really, whatever the leadership can dream up. The Chick-fil-A Bowl would manage. It spent $3.3 million in 2008 when flush with sponsorship money and lacking any incentive to watch expenses.

The 2008 Chick-fil-A Bowl—a nonprofit organization—turned a 16.9 percent profit. It couldn't waste its way to break-even, ending the year $2,073,747 in the black. Rather than give extra to the colleges that could use it or offer more to charity, the bowl put the profits into reserves. It ended the fiscal year with $15.7 million in total assets, including $8.1 million in cash.

This is an enterprise well capable of dealing with postseason competition and is primed to live as long as Methuselah. However much Cartel Kool-Aid Delany and Hancock consume, they cannot look at the Chick-fil-A Bowl and envision it disappearing.

"Of course bowl games are going to survive," Mountain West Conference commissioner Craig Thompson said. "If you

understand the business, you know the bowls are not going to
go away if a playoff is implemented."

Know this about the bowl system: It is not subject to a free
market, and this is where the future of the smaller bowls comes
into play. If left alone, the minor bowls would collapse, and they
would collapse spectacularly.

The BCS operates much like a government, offering a form
of welfare to ensure the survival of small bowls. Industry in-
siders estimate just fourteen of the thirty-five current bowl
games are self-sufficient. The rest profit from a system that takes
money from universities and guides it into the pockets of bowl
operators.

It's more shell game than bowl game. Take Minnesota, which
agreed to buy 10,500 full-price tickets to the 2008 Insight Bowl
in Tempe, Arizona, according to records the school filed with the
NCAA. When Minnesota sold only 1,512, it incurred a $434,340
loss on tickets alone. It spent an additional $1.2 million on travel
costs and other expenses. In the end, it cost Minnesota $1.7
million to collect the bowl's $1.2 million payout. In a vacuum,
Minnesota's bowl experience would have been at least a half-
million-dollar financial drain.

Power conference teams are willing to lose money on smaller
bowls because their league peers cover the losses by participating in BCS games with $19.8 million payouts. The Big Ten pooled
its bowl payout money and cut Minnesota a check that covered
nearly all of its expenses.

Meanwhile, the Insight Bowl enjoyed its guaranteed ticket
revenue. Despite close to 25,000 empty seats, it turned nearly a
$1 million profit, according to tax records. In essence, the Rose
Bowl funded the Insight Bowl. This is how the system works.

As long as the Big Ten agrees to an arrangement that cuts into its big-game profits, small games will go on forever. If the Insight Bowl operated in a real marketplace, Minnesota wouldn't play in a game that required it to pay its own way for nearly a week or buy full-price tickets it can't sell. In 2009, the bowl drew an anemic 0.4 television rating. Left to make an honest living, the Insight Bowl would likely wither and die.

This doesn't bother the Cartel. Actually, quite the opposite. It keeps adding games that can't stand on their own. Maybe it's because athletic directors receive bonuses for bowl appearances. Or because coaches use bowl appearances to fetch contract extensions. Or because conference commissioners push their salaries into the multimillions by citing, among other things, how many of their teams participated in a bowl. Or because none of the suits want to give up the lavish lifestyle provided by bowls: the dinners and the drinks, the golf outings, and the entertainment.

"A few years ago, our ADs came to me and said, 'You've got to start some bowl games,'" Thompson said. "I said, 'You're going to lose money.' They said, 'I don't care.'"

Thompson obliged. Of the Mountain West's five bowl affiliates, one started in 2003, another in 2005, and one more in 2006. New bowls are birthed nearly every year, all happy to be the newest Insight Bowl, a loser the system turns into a winner.

The Insight Bowl and others like it aren't alive because of tremendous business acumen. They exist because the Cartel says they should. The Cartel could pull the plug on 60 percent of the bowls tomorrow if it wanted. Since it doesn't, these games—fundamentally flawed businesses—end up like factories with a government contract.

Most fans couldn't care less if a smaller bowl peters out. No one will protest outside 1600 Pennsylvania Avenue if the Eagle-Bank Bowl goes under. The Cartel nevertheless contends that the monetary losses, no matter how outrageous, are well worth it because they allow players, coaches, and athletic-department officials to have a "positive experience." Hancock, the BCS executive director and once head of the NCAA men's basketball tournament, said playing in a minor bowl game is a superior experience to March Madness. "It's an awesome thing," Hancock told radio host Dan Patrick.

If the Cartel believes money is immaterial and funding bowl games is a worthwhile expense, that's great. It guarantees that the bowls will never die. Especially not with a playoff, which would generate enough money to fund bowl games until the end of time.

Currently, the payouts for the thirty-five bowl games are worth about $220 million to college teams. This is the total gross revenue the postseason produces for the schools. About $80 million of that is spent on travel, unsold tickets, and bonuses. It's the cost of doing business in the bowl system, the money that keeps the smaller bowls alive.

While exact figures are impossible to count because of the disparity between listed and actual payouts and the participation of private schools that aren't required to release financial information, the entire system generates a profit of around $140 million for the schools.

If the Cartel doesn't mind spending $80 million to subsidize bowl games when the gross revenue is $220 million, it isn't going to suddenly pull the plug when a playoff generates $750 million. Governments don't cut the welfare rolls when tax revenue almost quadruples. Even if bowl payouts dipped 50 percent and generated just $110 million, as they could, the money would be a drop in the bucket as long as a playoff is around.

College football would be replacing a poor earner with a good one. Spending $80 million of $860 million in revenue is infinitely more palatable than $80 million of $220 million. If the Cartel has no problem allocating 36.4 percent to keep all these bottom-tier bowls now, it would be thrilled to pay just 9.3 percent.

Either way, the dead bowls, universally accepted through the years as a consequence of a playoff, are merely a myth. As long as the BCS isn't inclined to commit bowl hara-kiri, the games will live long, fulfilled lives. Unless one of the Cartel's closest allies smartens up and goes turncoat.

Brains are the only real threat to bowl games. The system is safe until a conscientious president looks at the financial disaster that is the majority of bowls, starts asking questions, and sees what the bowl system hath wrought.

"The lower bowls are only susceptible because conferences might recognize that investment in bowls can no longer be justified," Western Athletic Conference commissioner Karl Benson said. "A playoff could allow more scrutiny and more assessment as to what is really a good business deal. So many bowls are bad business deals."

It would take a group of BCS-conference schools to realize they're paying for those bowl cocktail parties, an independent-thinking faction of presidents to take on the Cartel and proclaim it has twenty better places to spend $1.7 million than on some bowl with a 0.4 TV rating in Arizona.

That day could be approaching. *USA Today* reported in January 2010 that Division I-A athletic departments collectively needed $826 million in subsidies from taxpayers and student fees to balance their books. The NCAA says colleges dropped

227 teams between 2007 and 2009, mostly due to budget short-falls. The Knight Commission on Intercollegiate Athletics released a study in October 2009 that detailed the concerns of university presidents on those rising athletic costs. The report featured input from presidents representing 80 percent of Division I schools.

The commission concluded "university presidents at institutions with major football programs agree that current spending trends on intercollegiate athletics cannot be sustained nationally and collective action is needed to address escalating costs."

It is the impetus behind the expansion of the NCAA men's basketball tournament to sixty-eight teams as well as waves of conference realignments that could end historic rivalries. The people that run college athletics will spit in the face of their traditions. They just won't mess with the Chick-fil-A's.

The current bowl system isn't coming close to meeting the financial needs of its athletic departments. If ever the presidents took collective action, the Welfare Bowls would make a prime target. Cutting out bottom-tier bowls would improve profits. The extra money could go to scholarships, improvements around campus, or even other sports instead of covering a trip for the football team to SeaWorld. Maintain the status quo, and the risk that bowls die is far greater than if a playoff comes to fund them for eternity.

It's painful to learn the abject shadiness of bowl games, from their backdoor deals to their outrageous executive salaries to their fudged payouts to their selfish priorities. Bowls, as a business, stink. And yet there's something innately good about them that muffles and ultimately mutes the shock: The football itself. Bowls are great because of the players and the coaches and the action and the excitement. The most compelling drama may be in the Rose Bowl one year and the Beef 'O' Brady's St. Petersburg Bowl the next. The game doesn't discriminate. It always conquers. It deserves the best system possible, one whose weekdays teem with bowls and whose weekends sizzle with playoffs, a monthlong cornucopia of college football madness.

Something that's positively alive.

8 It's Always Some Team Getting Screwed

In the weeks leading up to the 2005 national championship game, an e-mail chain circulated among a group of friends in the South. They were rabid Louisiana State football fans, the kind who write the word "go" with a Frenglish twist—*Geaux Tigers!*—and want to canonize Billy Cannon. They were angry. And they vowed revenge.

The ringleader was a man named Steve Cospolich. He was a twenty-six-year-old Internet consultant. He and his buddies scoffed at what they were hearing ad nauseam on ESPN: that USC, which would face Texas at the Rose Bowl in the BCS title game, was primed to win its third consecutive championship.

"They kept saying threepeat," Cospolich said, "and I wanted to know how you can have a threepeat if you don't even have two."

Just how many championships USC has won this millennium continues to be a matter of dispute. When it comes to the BCS, no one is ever really certain. It's not just small schools begging for access. It's not just unbeaten teams complaining about getting shafted. It's the actual BCS champion getting forgotten, and it happened to LSU in 2003.

At the end of that regular season, the Tigers were chosen to face Oklahoma in the BCS title game despite USC's superior ranking in the Associated Press and coaches' polls, both of which factored in the BCS formula. LSU and Oklahoma each had better computer ratings, even after the Sooners' embarrassing Big 12 Championship game loss to Kansas State, and that particular incarnation of the BCS formula failed to reward a dominant USC team whose sole defeat came in triple overtime at Cal. On January 4, 2004, LSU beat Oklahoma to win the BCS title. The Tigers were college football's official champion.

USC, meanwhile, romped over fourth-ranked Michigan. The writers voted the Trojans an overwhelming No. 1, and they received the unofficial title of people's champion. So impressive was USC that three coaches—obligated by contract to vote the BCS title-game winner No. 1—went rogue and chose the Trojans instead. President George W. Bush invited USC and LSU to the White House. The next year, USC went undefeated and was the undisputed champion, and it had run the table leading up to the 2006 championship game as well.

So when Texas upset USC 41–38 in the game of the decade, Cospolich and his friends hooted, hollered, and hatched their plan. There was no threepeat. In their minds, the Trojans didn't even have a repeat. One day after Texas's win, Cospolich and some friends launched a Web site called Onepeat.com. It was embarrassingly simple: a Photoshopped graphic poking fun at USC and, as a joke, a PayPal link next to it encouraging donations to fund a billboard in Los Angeles that needled Trojans fans. Cospolich figured he'd circulate it among LSU fans, catch a few laughs, and move on.

Something happened. One friend forwarded it to a few others. And those people passed it along to their buddies. And thus was born one of the biggest viral crazes to hit college football, one that resulted in a hundred thousand people dropping by Onepeat every day and that benign PayPal logo getting a serious workout.

Money poured in. Not just from Louisiana, either. A lawyer

in Texas sent in $1,000. UCLA fans relished the chance to embarrass their nemesis. Even Notre Dame faithful supported Onepeat's cause. Cospolich did interviews on radio stations across the country. The New Orleans *Times-Picayune* splashed ONEPEAT across its front page. Within ten days, Cospolich had raised more than $10,000, and he had enough for his billboard campaign.

Five years later, as he looks back on his little contribution to college football history, Cospolich laughs. Onepeat was a success, no question, stirring the masses like any good BCS-related propaganda. It also reminded him of something that no LSU fan, nor the Cartel, really cares to acknowledge: Any national championship that needs ten grand and a billboard to legitimize it probably isn't worth a damn anyway.

"It's always some team getting screwed," Cospolich said.

This is the first time he has gone public with his full name. He figures the USC contingency that filled his e-mail inbox with vile letters has calmed down, and that no one would want to hurt a father of two-year-old twins. And anyway, Cospolich and the rest of the Onepeat brain trust—Shawn Mayeux, Kris Chelette, and Cory Cochran—want a little bit of credit for reminding people that the BCS doesn't limit its damages to college football's guppies.

For a system with one distinct mission—"It is nothing more than [an] attempt to match the No. 1 and No. 2 teams," according to the official BCS Web site—it is rather awful at its job. Of the twelve national championship games since its inception, at least seven have provided questionable matchups.

Which is no surprise when the top two teams are determined by coaches who vote along political lines, Harris Poll electors with obvious regional biases, and computers whose influence is neutered by the restrictions the BCS places on them. In 2005, USC thrashed Oklahoma 55–19 in the biggest blowout in BCS title-game history. Meanwhile, another undefeated team that tore through the toughest conference in the country and finished the season undefeated could only watch and wince.

"It still kills me," said Tommy Tuberville, coach of the 2004 Auburn team that finished 13-0 after a flawless eight-game SEC season. "I coached (as an assistant) in five national championship games at Miami. I knew what kind of team we had at Auburn. We beat five top 15 teams that year. USC and Oklahoma played three total between them. It's just so much politics."

Tuberville's beef resonates just like Cospolich's and the millions of other grudges against the BCS. LSU can't claim a national championship it owns. Perfection couldn't buy Auburn the chance to play for one. Tuberville rattles off the list of players from that '04 team: Cadillac Williams, Ronnie Brown, Jason Campbell, Marcus McNeill, Carlos Rogers, Jay Ratliff—"as good a team as we ever had at Miami," said Tuberville, now in his first year as head coach at Texas Tech.

No matter the talent, Tuberville recognized the near impossibility of a national championship game before the season even started. In the first polls of 2004, the AP and coaches' voters placed USC at No. 1 and Oklahoma at No. 2. Auburn was 17th with the writers, 18th with the coaches. Neither USC nor Oklahoma lost during the regular season, and no matter how impressive Tuberville's Tigers were, the voters weren't going to endorse them over the Trojans or Sooners. Traditional powerhouses without a loss don't drop in the rankings. The computers agreed: None placed Auburn higher than third.

Auburn beat Virginia Tech in the Sugar Bowl, its consolation game, and Tuberville flew to Miami the next day to attend the Orange Bowl. Shortly before kickoff, he held a press conference to lobby voters to change their minds on Auburn. His populist appeal earned Auburn one first-place ballot in the AP poll despite USC's overwhelming win in the title game. The majority of voters listened, nodded along, and went back to the buffet, unmoved by Tuberville's speech that proved more prescient than convincing.

"This has created, and will continue to create, a lot of problems," he said that night, "when you have people determining a mythical national championship through polls and not having everyone play it out on the field. It's unfortunate that people won't get to see it played out like it should."

The wounds haven't healed in the years since. USC was later found guilty by the NCAA of major rules violations surrounding star running back Reggie Bush. One of the penalties was the vacating of the Orange Bowl victory over Oklahoma. The BCS has said it would review whether to strip the Trojans of their title once the school has exhausted its appeals. It won't, however, retroactively award the title to Auburn. It may turn out the Tigers were the country's only unbeaten team and still were shut out.

It was far from the first BCS mess. The cluster at the top of the polls in 2000 foretold future chaos. Undefeated Oklahoma was the unquestioned No. 1 team. The BCS chose Florida State over Miami as the No. 2 team, even though the Hurricanes were ranked higher by the human polls and had beaten the Seminoles head-to-head during the season. Miami cruised over Florida in the Sugar Bowl. Florida State managed a safety against Oklahoma in a 13–2 championship-game loss that would make a driver's-ed video look downright entertaining.

Even more egregious was 2001, when the BCS chose a team that didn't win its own division to play in the championship. Nebraska was undefeated through eleven games and inched its way to No. 2 in the polls before traveling to Colorado to lock up the Big 12 North title and a shot at the conference championship.

Over four embarrassing hours, Nebraska allowed 380 rushing yards, nearly 600 yards of total offense, and the most points in school history. Colorado kept running the same trap play, 98G, and the Nebraska defense regressed to Pop Warner level. Colorado running back Chris Brown scampered for six touchdowns, and that wasn't the worst part of the 62–36 loss. In everyone's mind—even Nebraska coach Frank Solich's—the national-championship possibility was dead. The *Los Angeles Times* speculated Nebraska would consider courting offers from the Cotton Bowl or Holiday Bowl.

Little did the Cornhuskers realize a pair of upsets would vault them right back to where they were, second in the BCS standings, .05 points ahead of the Colorado team that blitzed them, further proof that a loss is OK as long as . . . well, no one ever really figured out how a four-touchdown loss counted as a prerequisite for a national title–game appearance.

Oregon coach Mike Bellotti seethed. The Ducks, ranked second in both polls, were somehow fourth in the BCS standings, and they handily beat Colorado in the Fiesta Bowl. Bellotti had enough. He could no longer do the bidding of college football's powers that be and pretend like the BCS was a good idea. His evisceration of the system remains the angry standard for coaches.

"I liken the BCS to a bad disease, like cancer," Bellotti said. "Not to take anything away from Nebraska or Colorado—they're great football teams—but one has two losses and the other didn't win their conference championship. We're No. 2 in both polls, but those things don't have a lot of merit, obviously."

Very obviously with the 2003 USC team that finished the regular season ranked No. 1 in both polls, a number that looked especially promising after Oklahoma lost by four touchdowns in its final game leading up to bowl season. Kansas State handed out the whipping this time, scoring thirty-five unanswered points on the Sooners, and still, the BCS divined that Oklahoma and LSU would make for a better game than USC and LSU. It led Trojans quarterback Matt Leinart to conduct a nationally televised interview while wearing a T-shirt that read "F*ck the BCS." An entrepreneur started selling them online within weeks. Cospolich wasn't the only one to take advantage of the BCS backlash.

"I think it stinks," then-USC coach Pete Carroll said. "I don't think it's the way it should be. But all we can do is keep talking about it."

And talk they have, from Tuberville asking for votes in 2004 to Les Miles using slick phraseology to back LSU into the 2007 BCS championship game over a plethora of other two-loss teams. The talk continued with the 2008 Utah team never getting its shot at a championship despite an undefeated record.

"We basically have a system for college football that too closely resembles the old Soviet Presidium," Air Force coach Troy Calhoun said. "You have a . . . politburo that's decided if you aren't one of those party members, then you're unable to participate."

Then came 2009, when five teams entered the bowl season undefeated.

"There's really no true champion with the system that's in place," Utah coach Kyle Whittingham said.

"A change is imminent and necessary," Brigham Young coach Bronco Mendenhall said.

"You've got to blow it up and start over," Florida coach Urban Meyer once said, and remember that Meyer has won two BCS championships with the Gators. He also coached the 2004 Utah team that, along with USC and Auburn, finished the season un-defeated. Meyer has lived the ultimate joy the BCS delivers, and he still sees its flaws.

The anti-BCS consensus seems to build every year, although the American Football Coaches Association's release of its annual coaching poll would indicate otherwise. Last year, the AFCA claimed that 73 percent of coaches like the current system. That's a compelling number. Only the AFCA's choice of yes or no doesn't offer a reasonable alternative to the coaches—say, a well-designed sixteen-team playoff—which means the BCS is such a disaster that 27 percent of coaches would rather have nothing. Any legitimate pollster would mock such a biased survey.

"I was dead right," Tuberville said. "Sometimes I'll sit there and think, 'You will be the only team ever in the history of college football to go 13-0 in the SEC and not play for a championship.' I think we could've beaten USC. We'd played them hard the previous two years. We would have given them a game."

Just think: If Auburn had made the 2004 championship game, and if it had beaten USC, the college football world today would look mighty different. One of those changes would be in cyberspace, where Onepeat.com would be a domain name without an owner.

When the traffic died down and the donations stopped trickling in, the Onepeat gang counted the contributions: $11,625, more than enough to hang the billboard on 39th and Figueroa, next to the Los Angeles Memorial Coliseum and nearly kitty-corner from the USC campus. They had enough left over to order a car-hauled advertisement that drove around ESPN headquarters in Bristol, Connecticut, and reminded the network that its three-peat talk was nonsense.

Cospolich first worked out the finances. The L.A. billboard would cost about $5,000 and the mobile billboard around $4,000. They donated the remaining $2,625 to Hurricane Katrina victims, then went about the most important part of the plan: coming up with an effective slogan. Cospolich and his friends bandied about a few before settling on a simple, effective jab:

SHOULDN'T DYNASTIES WIN MORE THAN ONE?

The billboard went up February 23, 2006, and LSU fans celebrated their victory. A self-professed "fat-cat alum" from USC named Kevin Robl promised to outdo Onepeat's billboard with one of his own in Baton Rouge. Locals threatened to vandalize it, and an LSU fan said he wanted to burn down Robl's house. No one ever saw a pro-USC billboard.

A little more than a week after the Los Angeles billboard poked across the L.A. skyline, Cospolich dispatched the mobile billboard to the ESPN campus for two days. As cathartic as this was, the bitterness remained. Cospolich's school won the national championship, and he needed to argue with people on behalf of its legitimacy.

"Every single statistical category that existed, we were better," said Mayeux, now Cospolich's business partner in the Web site Dealoco.com. "It's a subjective thing by the media. We lost to a ranked team. They lost to an unranked team in triple-overtime. It's all about what someone thinks. USC was a great team. I don't doubt that. Just because they whined about it doesn't mean they're national champions.

"It's college football. It's fun. But don't think that every time I hear the words 'USC' and 'national champions' I don't cringe."

Mayeux, Cospolich, and the rest of the Onepeat crew do take solace in their fortunes following the '04 championship. USC doesn't have a title since. The Bush case may mean it officially didn't win any. Nopeat.com, anyone? Pete Carroll left last off-season for the NFL. LSU won its second national championship in five years in 2007.

By then, the Onepeat legend had permeated the purple-and-yellow crowd, and among the faithful, Cospolich was a hero, the guy everyone in the bar wanted to buy a drink. He fought for LSU and its crystal trophies, even if those titles were handed out by an organization that bastardizes the name of a championship.

"Whenever we go back to visit, there's always somebody who heard we were the Onepeat guys," Cospolich said. "And they love us."

Onepeat.com is still running strong. It details everything from what prompted the site, to when it launched, to a detailed story of the billboards. Robl, the USC alum, promised a site himself: USCdynasty.com. It does not exist.

9 Cowardice and Cupcakes

Former Michigan athletic director Bill Martin wanted something special for the opening game of the Wolverines' 2010 season. It would mark the unveiling of the renovated Michigan Stadium, a nearly quarter-billion-dollar facelift for the eighty-three-year-old Big House. Martin knew the historic date deserved a name opponent, not some weak Mid-American Conference team or, even worse, a nonentity out of Division I-AA.

He suspected some big-time schools would decline the opportunity. Still, Martin had a lot to offer. This was Michigan, after all, the winningest program in college football history. The game would be on national television. ESPN's *College GameDay* might show up. For recruiting purposes alone—the chance to play at one of the sport's great sanctuaries—it seemed a no-brainer.

Best of all, Martin was willing to do nearly anything, including return the game with a home date on the other school's campus. Michigan is the kind of opponent that drives ticket sales, excites alums, and draws high school prospects to town—"The Victors," the maize and blue, the winged helmet. This was Scheduling 101, Martin figured. Come to our place, we go to yours. Just about every school would jump at getting the iconic Wolverines for a home game, right?

Actually, wrong.

Martin worked the phones seeking any team from a major conference. Obviously, Florida, which hasn't played a regular-season, nonconference game outside of its home state since the BCS was created, wasn't going to sign on. Perhaps someone else from the SEC? Sorry. Maybe the Big 12? Or the Pac-10? Texas and USC might say no, but a team from the middle of the pack? Hello? Anyone?

Martin felt like he was listening to a two-year-old: no, no, no, he kept hearing. The open date on his schedule stared at him, and he couldn't conceive mighty Michigan turning into some sort of a beggar. "I thought the allure of playing in the opening game of renovated Michigan Stadium would be a big draw," Martin said.

By July 2009, Martin was scrambling. The Wolverines needed an opponent, and the best they could find was a Big East program that hadn't played at the Division I-A level until 2000. Martin was thrilled nonetheless, because at least the University of Connecticut wanted to come to Ann Arbor and play in front of 110,000 people. Of course, that was as much for the 2013 return game at 40,000-seat Rentschler Field—the smallest venue to host the Wolverines in "as long as we can remember," Martin said—as anything.

"We got someone from a BCS conference," Martin said amid complaints from fans. "The fans have no idea how difficult that is to do. I'm excited we could do it. It was very, very difficult."

Blame the BCS. The Cartel will tell anyone within earshot, over and over and over and over, that protecting the sanctity of the regular season is paramount and that a playoff would destroy it. Which is funny, because under the BCS the regular season has turned into something of a sham. College football succeeds despite the BCS, not due to its existence.

The BCS has gutted the regular season by rewarding teams for scheduling cupcake opponents in a blatant effort to either go undefeated or secure the six wins needed to guarantee bowl eligibility. September is a relative bore, and the days of coaches challenging their teams, seeking out national games, or offering value to their season-ticket holders is on life support when Michigan—Michigan!—can't even get a good game to reopen the Big House.

Because the polls reward teams with impressive records more than ones with impressive résumés, it discourages scheduling an early-season, out-of-conference challenge. Voters have proven over decades they gravitate toward glossy records, no matter the opponents. Almost always, a major-conference team going 12-0 with a weak schedule is considered better than an 11 1 team that went through a meat grinder. The shiny zero clouds the concept of quality wins. The Cartel knows this and endorses it. By not providing voting criteria or, even better, establishing an informed selection committee, the Cartel has, by inaction, created a system that continues to further drain the very regular season it claims so vital to the game's health.

To compete for a spot in the BCS title game, the road map is simple: Own a brand name and don't lose in the regular season. Texas didn't in 2009, and the Longhorns won the human vote ahead of undefeated Cincinnati, Texas Christian, and Boise State. Texas, jobbed by the BCS before, learned how to work the system perfectly.

"They don't penalize you for playing weaker teams," Martin said. "Would we love to play Texas? You bet we would. I'd schedule them right now. We would love to play the traditional schools. But that isn't how it works anymore."

Such apprehension is routine among top-tier schools. It extends to the mid-level programs that rejected Michigan. Even teams with no realistic shot at a BCS title have little incentive to schedule an opponent against which they may struggle.

Bowl games, the Cartel's partners in obstruction, now feature seventy schools, or nearly 60 percent of the 120-team Division I-A. Athletic directors and coaches, most of whom collect five- or six-figure bonuses for reaching a bowl game, make up schedules. Missing out on a bowl is employment suicide, an automatic public damning, proof that a football program, most athletic departments' breadwinner, can't even back its way into mediocrity.

So ADs and coaches schedule to survive. If a team can start the season with a 4-0 record penciled in thanks to weak opponents, it need go only 2-6 in conference play to qualify for a bowl. In the world of the BCS, that counts as success and merits a bonus. It's a low standard, something the Cartel embraces. Poll voters care about records, bowl operators care about selling their tickets, and nobody cares about the nonconference schedule.

Or better put: No guts, plenty glory. According to research by ESPN.com's Pat Forde, there were fifteen games in 1988 between nonconference teams ranked in the preseason top 20. In 2009, there were four. For the entire country. Over the entire season, which expanded from eleven to twelve games.

While the system encourages big-name teams to schedule cream-puff nonconference games, it also rewards teams such as Boise State, with its easier-to-navigate conference schedules. This has been an unintended consequence for the Cartel. Playing in the Western Athletic Conference and moving to the Mountain West in 2011, Boise's road to an undefeated season is far easier than if it played in the SEC or Big 12. It doesn't have to run the weekly gauntlet of mostly good-to-great opponents, dealing with the inevitable injuries, letdowns, and huge opposing stadiums. The Broncos' season boils down to one or two big nonconference games.

The BCS was designed to snuff out Boise State. It hasn't,

which leaves major conference schools griping about the Broncos' schedule. A playoff would end the problem, making Boise State earn a title-game bid like everyone else, which is how the school wants it.

Boise State, due to its growing reputation, runs into trouble scheduling out-of-conference powerhouses. Like Michigan, it's on a constant search for quality nonconference opponents, only to find unreturned calls. And so goes the cycle, with the small-conference giants bumping their heads on the ceiling while the big-conference teams get fat on their peers' reputations.

Consider the 2007 Kansas Jayhawks, a team coming off a 6-6 season that, by the program's standards, wasn't half-bad. They started the year with the following four nonconference opponents: Central Michigan, Florida International, Southeastern Louisiana, and Toledo, all at home. The Jayhawks rolled by a combined score of 214–23.

The queue of patsies—or, in this case, pastries—was so blatant that the *Lawrence Journal-World*'s Web site accompanied a story on the easy schedule with a picture of corpulent coach Mark Mangino and the headline: MANGINO: CUPCAKES SERVED THEIR PURPOSE.

The voters weren't laughing. They were too busy pushing the Jayhawks up the rankings. Due to a fortunate Big 12 schedule, Kansas didn't play Oklahoma, Texas, or Texas Tech that season. As they cruised through the season, the Jayhawks got to 11-0 without playing a single ranked team. Actually, forget ranked. They hardly played a winning team. Kansas beat just two Big 12 teams with above-.500 records: Texas A&M and Oklahoma State, both of which finished 7–6.

Yet prior to kickoff against Missouri in their regular-season finale, the Jayhawks were ranked No. 2 in the BCS standings. They had a clear path to the BCS title game. In a season where

clearly superior teams had lost one game, Kansas parlayed its
fortunate schedule into an unbeaten record, and beating lousy
teams amounted to worthiness. These cupcakes were actually
good for you.

Kansas wound up losing to Missouri and fell out of conten-
tion for the national championship. The Jayhawks did get a
berth in the Orange Bowl—ahead of the Tigers, in fact—and
acquitted themselves in victory. The point still resonated. Kansas almost parlayed a limp schedule into a shot for the title. Others copied the plan. Pride left college football's regular season
long ago.

It was once taboo to play a Division I-AA opponent. They
are sacrificial lambs, small schools happy to take a beatdown
from a Division I-A school in exchange for a six-figure payday.
Now only USC, UCLA, Notre Dame, and Washington haven't
played a lower-division school—and UW will lose its I-AA vir-
ginity in 2011. One I-AA opponent is the new norm, and two
isn't altogether frowned upon. If the voters and the bowl directors don't care, and the Cartel repeats its regular-season talking
point often enough that people start to believe it, schools will
dive through loopholes.

Twenty-three percent of nonconference SEC games are now
against I-AA foes, according to research by Matt Hayes of *The
Sporting News*. The Big Ten plays 21 percent of its nonconference games against I-AA teams. Other conferences are just as
guilty. Fans still pay full price to watch the slaughter, of course.

In 2008, Texas Tech gladly scheduled a pair of I-AA opponents, started 10-0, and stayed in the chase for a BCS title bid
deep into November. Voters didn't care that its nonconference
slate featured Eastern Washington and Massachusetts. Being
unbeaten convinced the polls the Red Raiders were the country's fifth-best team before they had faced another ranked team.

Former Texas Tech coach Mike Leach, a Pepperdine law school graduate and one of the smartest coaches in America, essentially shortened the season to eight games with his I-AA opponents, plus Nevada and Southern Methodist. He had to know it didn't matter whom he played in the nonconference season. *Sports Illustrated* reported Tech turned down overtures from LSU and played Eastern Washington instead.

Certainly the 2008 Red Raiders and 2007 Jayhawks were legitimate, capable of posting similar records against quality teams. They simply chose not to, taking the expressway over the craggy terrain. The BCS doesn't delineate between cowardice and strategy. If unbeaten is the goal, might as well avoid trying to do it against twelve or thirteen major-conference opponents when eight will do. If every week is a playoff—as the Cartel wants the public to believe—there is no easier way to win the tournament than play a bunch of No. 16 seeds.

Former USC coach Pete Carroll saw scheduling in a different, refreshing way. He ran his program based on the idea of competition. He challenged his players in practice and tried to translate that to Saturdays. Carroll craved the chance to test his team in hostile environments against some of the nation's storied programs. In a move almost unheard-of anymore, he scheduled home-and-homes against major-conference teams and opponents of note: Ohio State, Auburn, Notre Dame, Nebraska, Colorado, Arkansas, and Kansas State, among others.

Under Carroll, the Trojans filled their pre-Pac-10 schedule with quality teams. According to *Sports Illustrated*'s Stewart Mandel, 73 percent of the Trojans' nonconference games came against BCS conference teams. The national average is 36 percent and dropping. The Trojans should be lauded and rewarded by the polls for doing what no other program does.

Instead, they're vilified. Following its 2005 title-game loss,

USC dropped games the next three seasons to huge underdogs. The stigma of Pac-10 letdowns followed the Trojans and
buried them in the polls. Rather than take practical off weeks
or shorten their schedule to nine Pac-10 games or cozy into the
L.A. Coliseum for the year, the Trojans faced a major-conference
opponent every week. They dodged more bullets. They dealt
with more injuries. They brought the allure absent everywhere
else in September. Yet they never got credit for the twelve-week
grind no one else dared to try.

Florida entered the 2009 season as the consensus No. 1 team,
coming off its second BCS title in three seasons with a loaded
roster. The Gators scheduled Charleston Southern, Troy, and
Florida International, along with their traditional game against
Florida State. Texas, a preseason top 5 team, set up games with
Louisiana-Monroe, Wyoming, Texas-El Paso, and Central Florida. Ole Miss, an upstart contender, followed Texas Tech's lead
and went with two I-AA directional schools (Northern Arizona and Southeastern Louisiana) to accompany Alabama-
Birmingham and Memphis. Penn State played home games
against Akron, Syracuse, Temple, and Eastern Illinois.

This begs for a solution. Saving the regular season, and protecting it from scheming ADs and coaches, demands a playoff
with at-large selections to guarantee that a loss wouldn't torpedo any team's season. Big-conference teams wouldn't fear a
nonconference challenge, as a defeat wouldn't slay their championship chances. Mid-tier teams would value victories against
bigger, badder opponents, knowing it would boost their chances
for an at-large bid. A selection committee told to value quality
of victory would reward the courageous, particularly when
considering seeds.

Teams would line up to play a home-and-home with
Michigan.

WEAKEST NONCONFERENCE SCHEDULES
FROM 2009 SEASON

Rutgers (9–4, won St. Petersburg Bowl)

Howard (2–9, I-AA): Won, 45–7
Florida International (3–9, Sun Belt): Won, 23–15
at Maryland (2–10, ACC): Won, 34–13
Texas Southern (6–5, I-AA): Won, 42–0
at Army (5–7, Independent): Won, 27–10

Northwestern (8–5, lost Outback Bowl)

Towson (2–9, I-AA): Won, 47–14
Eastern Michigan (0–12, MAC): Won, 27–24
at Syracuse (4–8, Big East): Lost, 37–34
Miami (Ohio) (1–11, MAC): Won, 16–6

Ole Miss (9–4, won Cotton Bowl)

at Memphis (2–10, Conference USA): Won, 45–14
Southeastern Louisiana (6–5, I-AA): Won, 52–6
UAB (5–7, Conference USA): Won, 48–13
Northern Arizona (5–6, I-AA): Won, 38–14

Penn State (11–2, won Capitol One Bowl)

Akron (3–9, MAC): Won, 31–7
Syracuse (4–8, Big East): Won, 28–7
Temple (9–4, MAC): Won, 31–6
Eastern Illinois (8–4, I-AA): Won, 52–3

Texas Tech (9–4, won Alamo Bowl)

North Dakota (6–5, I-AA): Won, 38–13
Rice (2–10, Conference USA): Won, 55–10
at Houston (10–4, Conference USA): Lost, 29–28
New Mexico (1–11, Mountain West): Won, 48–28

Kansas (5–7, did not qualify for bowl)

Northern Colorado (3–8, I-AA): Won, 49–3
at UTEP (4–8, Conference USA): Won, 34–7
Duke (5–7, ACC): Won, 44–16
Southern Miss (7–6, Conference USA): Won, 35–28

Instead, the Wolverines get UConn and we get the BCS playing the regular season's white knight when it's really the angel
of death. All the bloviating comes from the same Cartel suits
who knowingly deaden the schedule and make it such that a
game at the Big House is considered a bad thing.

"I'm concerned, because I just don't see the strength-of-
schedule philosophy being shared by as many people as we would
hope if we're really concerned with the health of college football,"
Oklahoma athletic director Joe Castiglione, one of the nation's
more aggressive schedulers, told ESPN.com. ". . . There are some
things on the horizon that make some of us wonder if it's a disin-
centive to scheduling harder nonconference games."

That's not protecting the sanctity of the regular season.
That's ruining it.

10 Diluting the Regular Season

In the final weeks of the 2009 NFL season, the Indianapolis Colts eschewed the pursuit of a perfect record to protect the health of their best players. They had clinched home-field advantage in the playoffs and didn't want a freak injury to torpedo their Super Bowl chances. So in late December against the New York Jets, quarterback Peyton Manning and others left in the third quarter with a lead and sat on the bench as the Colts blew the game and their unblemished season. A firestorm brewed soon thereafter, with Colts president Bill Polian and coach Jim Caldwell deemed pariahs for treating a potential 19-0 season as inconsequential. Fans across the country were merciless in their assessment: this was an awful way to end a season.

Of course, the Cartel was thrilled by the Colts' decision to tank. Off went a lightbulb in its collective head, albeit one that shone with the false glow of ignorance. Somehow, the Cartel came up with this argument against a playoff: If a team like Indianapolis is throwing games, how long until Ohio State just gives up against Michigan because its spot in the college tournament is set?

There are dozens of reasons this would never happen in college football, and the Cartel knows them all. It chose to exploit the Colts anyway, never allowing the truth to get in the way. The Cartel willfully ignored a reality borne out by history:

Not only has a scenario never arisen in which it would make mathematical sense for a team to sandbag games if there were a playoff, it never will. Ever.

Not that the Cartel would allow such fly-by-night disciplines as math or history to stop its scare tactics. The Colts' argument, fallacious though it may be, is a centerpiece to the talking point that a playoff would irreparably harm the sport's regular season. Never mind that the weekly drama leading up to a sixteen-team, fifteen-game college football bonanza would be palpable, the number of critical games would multiply, and schools big and small would benefit. More games would matter, and they would matter more.

Anyone with a simple understanding of probability knows that Indianapolis' decision doesn't have any relation to what could or would happen in college football. That didn't stop BCS executive director Bill Hancock from sending out lengthy press releases and blog posts arguing the exact opposite.

"[The Colts' decision] does offer a real-life illustration of what an NFL-style playoff could do to college football's regular season," Hancock wrote, before going on to argue against the laws of arithmetic.

Here's a real-life illustration for the Cartel: The Colts compete with fifteen teams for the No. 1 seed in the AFC. Each team plays sixteen games and, barring a tie, overall record is the sole seeding criteria. In a college football playoff, 120 teams would vie for the No. 1 seed. Their bodies of work are twelve or thirteen games. The seeds would be based on myriad factors: record, strength of schedule, quality of victory, and how and when a team lost.

Only one scenario exists in which a college team would consider throwing its final game under a playoff system: If a team is undefeated, and if every other team in college football has at least two losses, the undefeated team could conceivably lose its final game and keep the top seed. Of course, since the Associated Press first began crowning national champions in 1934, this has never happened. While records are a bit spotty dating all the way back to the first Princeton-Rutgers game in 1869, it doesn't appear to have occurred at any time in college football's 131-year history.

In the NFL, where the thirty-two franchises' schedules are similar, teams often jump to a two-game advantage in the standings because they play sixteen times and compete for division titles with three teams. A college football team would need to take a two-game lead over 119 others, and do so while playing 20 to 25 percent fewer games. It's essentially impossible.

And even if somehow a team defied all known principles of applied math, it would need a coach willing to insult his players, anger his alumni, and butcher his recruiting while hoping the selection committee wouldn't ding the team for a late-season loss.

In reality, the chances for sandbagging are far greater under the current system than in the Cartel's world. Because of the small number of teams competing for conference and division titles, the disproportionately large number of league games, and record being the only factor in determining league supremacy, it's common for teams to clinch either a league title or a berth in their conference title game with one or two regular-season appearances to spare.

For the teams that lost early in the season and have no hopes of making the BCS title game, they have reached their pinnacle: either a BCS bowl bid or a shot at the conference-championship game that gives them a chance at a BCS bowl. Technically, nothing prevents them from resting their starters in the final week. It could mean the difference between the Fiesta Bowl and the Insight Bowl.

Consider Ohio State in 2009. By mid-November, the Buckeyes had wrapped up the Big Ten title and a guaranteed a bid to the Rose Bowl. With two losses, however, they had no shot at the BCS championship leading into their game against archrival Michigan. By Hancock's reasoning, the game was meaningless, a sandbag special. The Buckeyes went all out, of course, because rivalries are rivalries—and their coach, Jim Tressel, didn't want his house torched. They weren't the only ones. Georgia Tech and Central Michigan had no bowl-based incentive to win their regular-season finales, either, and could have rested starters to prepare for their conference-title games. Neither team did.

Under the BCS, Hancock's supposed "real-life illustration" of potential tanking isn't just possible. It happened three times last year. Under a playoff, its likelihood drops to infinitesimal. A playoff doesn't create the problem. It actually eliminates it. Yet the Cartel spits at historically proven, mathematically based, logically thought-out fact. And it wonders why fans don't believe anything it says.

If the Cartel really is concerned about college teams pulling a 2009 Colts, it should eliminate automatic bids to BCS games for conference champions and base all selections on the final BCS standings. After that, perhaps it can move onto more likely calamities, like what to do if a blizzard hits the Orange Bowl.

The regular season is a bellwether issue for the Cartel, and so when one of its arguments rings hollow, it goes to its bag of half-truths and misdirection for another. Each holds as much water as a thimble, none more than the classic Cartel trick of making the BCS look prudent next to other sports.

The Cartel, for example, insinuates that men's college basketball—the NCAA's second most-popular sport—is a mess before March Madness, and a playoff would be just as ruinous for college football. "You look at college basketball, and I would say there's probably one must-see game during the regular season, Duke–North Carolina," Big Ten commissioner Jim Delany told *USA Today.*

While Tom Izzo and Thad Matta must appreciate their commissioner disparaging their programs, the greater point is: One of the most powerful men in college athletics compared two sports that are wildly dissimilar.

The men's basketball tournament boasts a field of sixty-eight, making entry fairly easy for major schools. The six big conferences have seventy-three teams playing basketball. Between their own automatic bids and thirty-seven at-large spots, they compete for forty-three available slots in the NCAA tournament. The rest go to champions of smaller conferences. That means 58.9 percent of major programs can potentially make the field. In 2009, for example, 49.3 percent (thirty-six teams) qualified for the then sixty-five-team tournament.

Those same six conferences have sixty-six football teams, including Notre Dame. A maximum of eleven teams (16.6 percent) could make a playoff. Football's regular season would be a survival of the fittest, while basketball's amounts to a survival of the slightly out of shape.

Basketball teams play between thirty and thirty-four pre–NCAA tournament games, nearly three times the size of a football schedule, automatically diminishing any single result. Teams play as many as four times a week, which weakens the build-up to any one game. Archrivals face each other two or three times a year, not once, like in football. Conference tournaments allow a last-chance shot at an automatic bid even for cellar dwellers. And for the teams that do succeed in the regular season, the tournament rewards high seeds marginally: no home-court advantage and only a slightly easier tournament draw that, after the first round or two, is a wash.

Football is apples. Basketball is oranges. Delany needs new taste buds.

No matter how much the Cartel tries to win the regular-season argument, it can't, because its central premise—under the BCS, every week of the season is a playoff—amounts to nothing more than a marketing line.

Which regular-season game eliminated Boise State, Cincinnati, and Texas Christian from the 2009 playoff? None. Who knocked Utah out in 2008? Nobody. What sort of playoff leaves out an undefeated team from the nation's best conference, as happened with Auburn in 2004? Eliminating unbeaten teams doesn't fit most definitions of a playoff.

Nor does one that allows teams back in after they lose. In 2007, Illinois beat Ohio State in November. It was supposed to kill the Buckeyes' chance of playing in the BCS championship game. Two weeks later, Louisiana State lost its regular-season finale to Arkansas. Gone, theoretically, were the Tigers' title hopes. The Cartel smiled. The every-week-is-a-playoff gambit looked smart.

Until January 7, that is, when the two teams that took the field at the Superdome in the BCS title game were Ohio State and LSU. Turns out every week is a playoff . . . except when it isn't. Like in 2001, when Colorado pasted Nebraska by twenty-six points in their regular-season finale and the Cornhuskers played for the national championship despite not owning their conference title. Not to be outdone, Oklahoma lost the Big 12 title game by twenty-eight points two years later and advanced to the BCS championship game.

A real playoff brings meaning back to September, adds excitement to October, and turns November into a footballpalooza where otherwise-obscure games draw widespread interest. Suddenly the MAC title game would be worth watching, because the winner becomes a first-round upset candidate. That's good for fans of the MAC and good for fans of college football. And, yeah, they're probably (Florida) Gator bait. Doesn't matter. The game will attract a crowd, the winning fans will storm the field like they won the national title, and they'll head to the biggest spectacle in college football instead of a lower-tier bowl.

Not just the smaller conferences benefit. The ACC title game, plagued by weak attendance, low ratings, and irrelevance under the BCS, would matter to everyone with a playoff. In 2009, fans of bubble teams would have tuned in to see whether Georgia Tech would win the league's automatic bid or lose and drop into the pool for one of the five at-large spots. When a real playoff plan is implemented, the implications of every game—from the ACC and Big East to the MAC and Mountain West—are far-reaching.

The chase for the five at-large bids would create a national free-for-all. The interlocking fortunes would take what people currently see as the thrill of college football and amplify it times ten. Any given Saturday in November currently provides four or five games with national implications. Imagine dozens of games, all intertwined, the fortunes of every bubble school shifting by the possession. Scores would change, scenarios evolve, fortunes rise and fall, all too fast for ESPN's Rece Davis to dream up enough subtle one-liners.

It's beautiful, this crescendo of college football, and all before the truest action begins in December. Instead of trying to embrace it, the Cartel comes up with every excuse possible, flimsiness no deterrent.

"You'd have a horrible argument over those [at-large bids]," former Pac-10 commissioner Tom Hansen told Dennis Dodd of

CBSSports.com, and how very rich that one of college football's great obstructionists talks about horrible arguments. The BCS is a Jenga tower of horrible arguments, each piece so very easy to pick out, the foundation getting shakier and shakier. An educated selection committee would have some difficult decisions, sure, but it's silly to equate the fight over the sixty-eighth team in the men's basketball tournament with the final at-large bid in a football playoff. A better question: What's worse, fighting over which two-loss team to invite to the football playoff, or coming up with a way of explaining to an undefeated major-conference team why it wasn't worthy to compete for the national title?

Even with five undefeated teams heading into bowl games, the 2009 regular season was a snoozer. All of the perfect teams played uninspired schedules, and the intrigue came only from upsets and the SEC title game between Alabama and Florida. One Saturday in November, none of the top nine teams in the BCS standings were less than a twenty-three-point favorite in Vegas. ESPN.com declared 2009 the season designed by Bernie Madoff.

"I don't want to see the regular season turned into a seeding process," Delany said.

Because . . . he's OK with de rigueur I-AA opponents? Or does Delany like the least compelling possible matchups? Delany's close-mindedness reflects the Cartel's aversion to a regular season worth having. By seeding the teams and offering home-field advantage to the best eight, the push to get to the top would create a secondary market of must-watch games.

The top 2 would have the right to host through the national semifinals. The top 3 teams would assume a traditionally easier first-round matchup against the Sun Belt, MAC, and Conference USA champions. The top 4 would get at least two home games and the top 8 one. Each step of the ladder is one more goal to pursue, one more race on which followers would fixate. While it seems impossible to make such games as Ohio State–Michigan, Auburn-Alabama, or Florida–Florida State more exciting, the fight for seeding would add that new dimension.

That's the thing about a playoff: It wouldn't just add opportunity or excitement to the postseason. It doesn't simply crown a champion. It reinvigorates the regular season, from the meaningful September to the exciting October to the wild November and on to the December and January that college football fans deserve.

11 Nonsense Math

Four years ago, a man named Hal Stern invited the nerds of the world to unite. Their enemy wasn't the typical scourge of jocks or acne but a faceless, inanimate entity that posed a threat to the credibility of all mathematicians.

Yes, the horror of the BCS extends beyond the sporting universe and into that of the bespectacled and pocket-protected. In an obscure math journal, Stern wrote an impassioned plea to the men whose ranking systems compose the computerized portion of the formula that determines who plays in the BCS championship game: Don't allow the Cartel to corrupt you and the laws of mathematics.

"I am advocating a boycott of the Bowl Championship Series by all quantitative analysts," Stern wrote in his 2006 article, which has earned a cult following after the godfather of modern sports statistics, Bill James, jumped on the boycott bandwagon and urged his peers to do the same. Along for the ride are dozens of other analysts who make up an underground subculture fascinated with ranking college football teams in their spare time.

They wonder why the six chosen systems bother abiding by draconian BCS rules. The computer rankings, for example, are not allowed to take into consideration margin of victory. A 63–0 victory is the same as a 6–3 win. Jeff Sagarin, the most famous of the computer rankers, calls his BCS rankings the "politically correct" version and says they're "less accurate" than another version he calculates. It includes margin of victory, and the Cartel won't allow him to use it.

"You're asked to rank teams that don't play each other, that don't play long seasons, and you can't include margin of victory?" said Kenneth Massey, another of the handpicked mathematicians, who also provides a "better version" on his Web site. "It's a very challenging problem from a data-analysis standpoint. It does require sacrificing a bit of accuracy. It's not the best way to do it."

The entire point of the BCS using computerized ranking systems was to provide some sort of impartiality and balance out the two human polls. The computers count for one-third of a team's BCS score. Of course, the first time they tried, the computers didn't jibe with the humans, so the Cartel changed the formula three years after the BCS started. Same for the second time the computers failed to agree with the voters. And the third. When the math didn't satisfy its standards—prop up the big schools, stomp on the small ones—the Cartel altered the formula.

"Stern's analysis was clearly right," said James, whose revolutionary work with baseball statistics was highlighted in the book *Moneyball* and who has since developed his own college football rating system. "This isn't a sincere effort to use math to find the answer at all. It's clearly an effort to use math as a cover for whatever you want to do. I don't even know if the people who set up the system are aware of that. It's just nonsense math."

The Cartel says it wants a fair and unbiased component. Instead, it's got another mess on its hands, one that turned into a talking point at the highest level of American politics. On November 3, 2008, the night before the presidential election,

Barack Obama appeared on *Monday Night Football*. He used the forum to reiterate a number of his positions. He also established a new one.

"I am fed up with these computer rankings," Obama said.

Obama's frustration was typical populist rhetoric. He didn't expound on why he disliked the computer rankings. He just disliked them. Truth is, the computers themselves aren't altogether terrible, certainly not the overwhelming problem. The bigger issue is the system under which they operate, and how ignoring something so telling as margin of victory is far from the only blunder.

Take the actual computing itself. Every week, the six systems input scores, let the computers spit out the rankings, and send them to the BCS. That's it. Nobody at the BCS doublechecks the rankings. Only one of the six, Wes Colley, makes his formula fully public. Which leaves five systems open for corruption with no safety net. Massey once admitted that if offered $1 million to doctor his standings, "It would take a lot of willpower to refuse that, to be sure." Rich boosters, forget that tailback recruit. Pool your money for this guy.

Massey earned a Ph.D. at Virginia Tech and now teaches mathematics at Carson-Newman College, and he's not the only scholar of the group. Sagarin is an MIT graduate who has ranked teams for *USA Today* since 1985, and Colley is a bowtie-wearing, Princeton- and Harvard-educated astrophysicist who tries to solve everyday problems like traffic and freight delays. Another doctor, Peter Wolfe, specializes in infectious diseases when he's not obsessing over college football, and political scientist Jeff Anderson and freelance sportscaster Chris Hester started compiling rankings from Hester's mother's computer twenty years ago.

Then there is Richard Billingsley. He is fifty-nine years old and lives in Hugo, Oklahoma. Unfailingly courteous, Billingsley speaks with a homespun voice that exudes calm. Though he's a stress-management expert for a living, Billingsley follows his passion for college football in obsessive ways. Starting in 1970, he set out to name a national champion for every season dating back to 1869, when Princeton and Rutgers split the two games played. (Billingsley's verdict: Princeton.) His institutional history of college football is unquestioned. There's just one snag.

"I'm not a mathematician," Billingsley said.

A nonmathematician who uses a numbers-based formula to rank teams. A nonmathematician who, accordingly, uses the previous year's rankings as a starting point for the next year's, even if a school graduates its quarterback, running back, and middle linebacker, and loses its coach.

"I don't know that the powers that be even know what he's doing," Stern said. "I'm not saying he's bad. But . . . he's bad. It's clear it's not what the BCS should be doing."

Billingsley is unrepentant about using the previous season's results. He believes the past portends the future, even if the past is now playing in the NFL. The other computer systems that use preseason rankings take into account graduations, recruiting classes, and coaching changes—everything that matters.

"I'm not even a highly educated man, to tell you the truth," Billingsley said. "I don't even have a degree. I have a high school education. I never had calculus. I don't even remember much about algebra. I think everyone questions everything I do. Why is he doing that? Does he know what he's doing, a crazy kook in Oklahoma? I had a guy tell me in an e-mail once that I'm a crazy Oklahoma hillbilly. Well, it's true, but it has nothing to do with my ranking skills."

The actual skill involved is suspect. A Dutch computer scientist named Martien Maas, who has never been to a college football game but compiles rankings in his spare time, analyzed amateur ranking systems for their accuracy in picking bowl games last year. He assumed the success rate of predicting the correct winners would be somewhere between 75 and 85 percent. The computers barely chose 50 percent of the games correctly.

And yet the Cartel insists the computers are integral to the BCS system. They've been around longer than any other ranking systems, even the AP. Stern grew up in New York and looked forward to reading the *Long Island Press* so he could study the Dunkel Index, a ranking system that predated the first computer by a decade. The original power poll, devised by Illinois professor Frank Dickinson, started sometime in the mid-1920s and was followed by Dartmouth professor Dick Houlgate's in 1927. Dick Dunkel arrived in 1929, and today his grandsons Bob and Richard continue computing the Dunkel Index for college football, the NFL, and even the CFL and WNBA.

The acceptance of independent, numbers-based analysis took years. When David Rothman, whose progressive rankings influenced Sagarin, wrote NCAA executive director Walter Byers asking that his system be adopted by the organization, he received the following response: "Mr. Rothman, we will never do standings at the NCAA and second, we will never do yours."

Byers retired in 1988. Ten years later, when the BCS was born, the system centered around three computer rankings: Anderson and Hester, Sagarin, and the *New York Times*. The next year, the BCS added Billingsley, Massey, Rothman, the Dunkel Index, and Herman Matthews. In 2001, it dumped the *Times* and Dunkel rankings and replaced them with Wolfe and Colley. A year later, Rothman and Matthews were gone after refusing to remove margin of victory from their formulas, and the BCS continued to impress Liz Taylor with its divorce rate.

The reasoning behind the decision to banish margin of victory before the 2002 season: The BCS didn't want teams that beat up on weaker opponents to be rewarded for doing so. Never mind that the BCS was actively corrupting the impartiality of its system. By mandating the removal of margin of victory, the BCS brought an issue patently tied to emotion—whether a blowout is right or wrong—into the machines it hired to be emotionless.

"Their action is crazy," Rothman told the *Cincinnati Enquirer*. "This makes the computer people look like hacks. It gives the impression of a lack of integrity."

To illustrate what he called "nonsense," Matthews removed margin of victory from the final rankings in which it was used, 2001, and sent the hypothetical results to the BCS. The starkest difference involved the University of Tennessee, which blew a chance at the national championship game by losing the SEC title to LSU and finished sixth in the BCS standings. It was Tennessee's second loss of the season, and yet without margin of victory, the Volunteers would have finished second in the BCS—ahead of one-loss teams from Nebraska and Oregon—and faced Miami in the championship game.

"That's really suspect," Matthews told the *Knoxville News Sentinel*. "Then Tennessee slaughtered Michigan (in the Citrus Bowl), but the Vols would have dropped from No. 2 to No. 3 while Michigan increased from No. 25 to No. 20. That's crazy."

All of this was in the name of sportsmanship, and nobody dislikes sportsmanship. The BCS neglected the numbers—the actual, objective data that a computer can measure—and the letters sent by Sagarin and Massey urging the BCS to allow them to keep their margin-of-victory rankings. It ignored the hypocrisy in letting the coaches and Harris Poll voters factor in margin of victory. It disregarded everyone who cares about the score of the game, which is pretty much anyone who watches. The computers were an easy scapegoat, and the BCS got rid of Rothman and Matthews because they refused to flout their mathematical principles.

Some of the computer rankers even parroted the illogical message.

"A significant but hard-to-measure factor in comparing teams is sportsmanship," Wolfe wrote on his Web site. "Running up the score is generally looked on as evidence of bad sportsmanship, behavior which should not be encouraged or rewarded."

The statistical community guffaws at Wolfe's concern with blowout victories while lamenting the BCS's decision. Any elementary mathematician, let alone someone with the ability to write a program that ranks every college football team, could figure out a way to limit margin of victory's effect—say, by making a thirty-point win count the same as a seventy-point win. *The American Statistician* in 2003 devoted more than five thousand words to how removing margin of victory compromised the rankings. The magazine's research showed the two best algorithms were Rothman's and Matthews', both discarded by the BCS.

"It's about respecting and accepting what the math tells you," James said. "If it tells you Boise State is better than the teams that have the opportunity to play for the championship, what are you going to do?

"Well, if Boise State ever finishes first, they'll change [the formula] a fourth time."

James isn't exaggerating. The BCS really has tweaked its formula three times. Its original version used computer rankings, human-poll rankings, a strength-of-schedule component, and number of losses. In 2001, the BCS added bonus points for quality wins. That wasn't good enough, so in 2002, it changed its quality-win formula and removed margin of victory. And after USC ended 2004 at No. 1 in the AP poll despite not playing for the BCS championship, the whole BCS system was blown up to de-emphasize the computers.

Fall guys once, fall guys always.

Even the mathematicians warned the Cartel the new system was untenable. "They looked at what we were trying to do and said . . . we're asking them to do an impossible job with imperfect tools," BCS consultant Kevin O'Malley told the Riverside (California) *Press-Enterprise*.

So, naturally, they went ahead with it anyway. The diluted computer rankings are determined rather simply. The six send in their twenty-five best teams, with the top one receiving twenty-five points and the lowest getting one point. For each team, the BCS drops the highest and lowest ranking to get rid of potential outliers, adds the four remaining numbers, divides them by a hundred to get a percentage, and averages that percentage with the one from the coaches' poll and Harris Poll.

The computer guys do it because they love the challenge of competing against other minds, sort of like a science fair for adults. Otherwise, the fringe benefits are fringy. It's a good conversation starter. It's a license to brag when you get something correct, like Anderson and Hester did in 2008, when they ranked Utah second before its bowl victory against Alabama. None of the other computers had Utah higher than fourth. Even the Utes' coach, Kyle Whittingham, voted them fifth.

It's not for the money. The BCS pays only a nominal sum, not close to enough for the rankers to quit their jobs. And it's not for the swag. Colley, a longtime Alabama fan, wanted to attend the 2009 SEC championship game between Florida and the Crimson Tide. He figured a couple tickets wouldn't be much trouble.

"I e-mailed the SEC BCS liaison," Colley said, "and he just laughed at me."

How fitting. The Cartel laughing at the computers. Its computers. The men who run the computer rankings for the BCS don't dare complain, their loyalty admirable if misguided, and that is where it goes wrong for Hal Stern, where any chance of the boycott dies.

To them, the computer rankings are a chance to matter, and that's something they hold on to dearly. They see it as a privilege, no matter how corrupt the organization, how shady the leadership, how unpopular it is—or they are—among fans. The fame and renown intoxicates them. The BCS chose them over more than a hundred others whose rankings appear on Massey's Web site, and it's good to feel important.

"We're part of history," Massey said, and he chewed on that idea for a moment, wondering whether it really is better to be a part of history that nobody supports than not to be part at all. He emerged from his quick philosophical debate with a compromise that seems downright shocking for someone employed by the BCS.

"I would like a playoff," Massey said.

He's not the only one.

"It's hard to argue with a sixteen-team playoff," Colley said.

Massey and Colley, and their ranking peers for that matter, are like so many others. They are good and smart people with noble intentions, and they work for bosses who make them look bad. The BCS is too strong a force. The nerds aren't ready for a revolution.

12 Fooling the Voters (Who Are Often Fools)

By the fourteenth year of their marriage, Kathy Miles understood what her husband, Les, needed after a devastating loss. She provided perspective amid his myopic self-loathing, the nurturing yin to his depressed yang. On this particular evening, one day after Thanksgiving in 2007, her attempt to comfort the Louisiana State football coach did more than work. With a little maternal optimism, Kathy Miles changed college football—and exposed another inherent flaw in the Cartel's system.

LSU had blown a clear shot at the BCS title game by losing, in triple overtime, to Arkansas. This was the regular-season finale, and even though LSU was still headed to the SEC championship game, the Tigers' national championship hopes were bleak. Their record was 10-2, and later that weekend, LSU fell from No. 1 to No. 7 in the BCS rankings.

In the history of the BCS, no team with two losses had ever played for the championship. Miles feared he'd have to listen to another off-season about how Saint Nick Saban, LSU's previous coach, would have gone undefeated with all this talent. Kathy tried to divert Miles's mind by reminding him that the Tigers' other defeat came in triple OT, too.

"You know, Les," she said, "you're undefeated in regulation."

Miles's ears perked up. Undefeated in regulation. It was brilliant.

To coaches, a loss is a loss. There are no moral victories. Miles played for Bo Schembechler at Michigan, and nobody dared classify a defeat as a good one. But Miles knew the majority of people who determine the national championship aren't coaches, and that in the BCS, a loss is a loss only if the voters punish you for it.

If LSU wanted back into the national title picture, all Miles had to do was convince voters it deserved a spot there. And so began the ingenious campaign that would change the way BCS titles are won in college football: through the power of marketing brains as much as on-field brawn. The Tigers weren't trying to jockey the system and deny a small school its chance for glory. LSU would hopscotch its big-conference brethren with the first intensive spin-doctoring of the BCS era.

The morning after his wife offered up the best-sounding college football slogan since Notre Dame made Joe Theismann change the pronunciation of his name to rhyme with Heisman— and that one didn't work—Les Miles shared the line with a man named Michael Bonnette. He is LSU's sharp-mined associate athletic director in charge of media relations, and Bonnette would soon prove the importance of public relations personnel, a mostly overworked and underpaid lot that is now immensely influential.

"I was impressed by the simplicity of the argument," Bonnette said. "We had to argue to people, 'Yeah, we've got two losses, but look how they came.'"

LSU understood it had no control over the computer formulas, which comprise one-third of the BCS formula that determines the title game. Miles and Bonnette targeted another Cartel weakness: the human polls, which make up the remaining two-thirds. The coaches' poll had sixty-one voters that year. The Harris Poll, a group of former college administrators, players, coaches, and media, had 114. And LSU was banking on the collective gullibility of those 173 men and two women to write its ticket to the championship game.

If the campaign gained traction and some other teams ahead of the Tigers in the BCS standings lost, they might slink back into the title-game discussion. It was a worthwhile Hail Mary, and Miles launched the plan during his weekly news conference.

"I like to talk about what we are and not what we lost," he said. "I look at a team that hasn't lost a game in regulation."

Plenty of eyes rolled. So did tape recorders, and reporters were more than happy to report Miles's assertion. He mentioned it again before the SEC title game in Atlanta, although his message was overshadowed by an erroneous report that he was about to become the head coach at Michigan. It was a nightmare for LSU, which wanted to stay on message.

LSU beat Tennessee that night, and the top two teams in the BCS standings, Missouri and West Virginia, lost. Miles immediately pounced, repeating his talking points. On the team's charter flight home, Bonnette worked the phones to key media and scored Miles a live interview on that night's *SportsCenter*. Back in Baton Rouge, Bonnette and his staff went to work on their propaganda. Bonnette believed the busy coaches and often-distracted Harris Poll voters wouldn't bother to digest more than a quick sound bite, if they even bothered to read their e-mails. And he suspected, quite accurately, that other schools had already drowned them in numbers with their appeals for title-game worthiness.

Instead, Bonnette put together a simple e-mail with four bullet points, the key being a central, emotional campaign slogan: "LSU is undefeated in regulation."

"We sold it," Bonnette said.

And the voters bought it in bulk. The Tigers, who had

beaten fourteenth-ranked Tennessee in the SEC championship game, jumped to No. 2 in both polls, and the computers concurred, giving them a second-place finish in the BCS rankings and assuring them a berth in the national championship game. A month later, they handily beat Ohio State for the title.

Les Miles held the crystal trophy. Kathy Miles cheered him on. Perhaps they should've switched places.

"I wish I could take credit for the line," Bonnette said.

While this wasn't the first major political push by a school, it indoctrinated the new era of unabashed, organized campaigns. Previously, teams relied on their conferences and broadcast partners to do their bidding. At halftime of the 2006 SEC championship game, with Florida ahead of Arkansas 17–7, SEC commissioner Mike Slive held a press conference and claimed that if the Gators won, they deserved the BCS title-game bid. "I'd be disappointed" if it didn't happen, he said. At the time, Slive was also serving as the BCS coordinator, which meant that the official head of the official postseason system officially admitted he might not agree with the official result.

CBS turned the second half into an unpaid advertisement for the Gators. Color commentator Gary Danielson used on-air graphics and his telestrator to make points on behalf of the conference that approves of him before he broadcasts its games. Danielson later told Detroit sports radio station WXYT he did it only because he felt ESPN/ABC was going to do the same promotion for Michigan of the Big Ten, with whom the network has a broadcast contract.

In the press conference following Florida's 38–28 victory, its coach, Urban Meyer, not only pumped up the Gators but compared them to the Wolverines. Michigan coach Lloyd Carr, whose idle team entered the week ahead of Florida in the two polls but had lost its regular-season finale to Ohio State, called that "inappropriate." Perhaps, but it was effective. Florida surpassed Michigan in both polls and the BCS standings, went to Glendale, Arizona, and trounced Ohio State for the national title. Michigan watched, in part, because it wasn't as committed to the P.R. fight.

By 2008, sportswriters covering a November game between Oklahoma and Texas Tech watched their e-mail in-boxes fill up during the second half with missives from the University of Texas showing how a Sooners victory would affect the Longhorns' BCS fortunes. The preemptive attack was a brushstroke of the modern media game. Texas just didn't play it well enough. After OU handily won, Sooners coach Bob Stoops didn't dwell on the satisfying victory. He launched into a campaign spiel on why Oklahoma should get picked over the Longhorns, who earlier in the season had beaten the Sooners. OU went to its fourth championship game of the decade.

The in-house scheming increases by the season. Some schools have begun setting up mini–war rooms with interns monitoring the Web so they can counter arguments made on obscure blogs and fan message boards. The resources allocated to BCS politicking are approaching the levels devoted toward Heisman Trophy campaigns.

Coaches are uncomfortable with this new job requirement. Mack Brown of Texas said he longs for the days when a postgame press conference was about discussing a great victory, not trying to spin voters. "You can't just look at the end all the time," Brown said. "That's what the system is making everybody do. They're not enjoying the season."

Precious few coaches try to avoid the BCS clamor, and it's toughest for those like Boise State's Chris Petersen, whose Broncos finished the season undefeated three times and still weren't deemed worthy of the title game. Petersen refuses to politick—

"It's never good enough," he said—and so the school and the Western Athletic Conference decided to do it for him. Last year, they hired a local public relations firm to make the case Boise State deserved a major bowl bid.

The BCS had created the sporting version of the Iowa primary. And like anything that deals with a popular vote, the populace can be mind-numbingly dumb.

In 2005, the Associated Press, which runs the oldest and most respected college football poll, told the BCS it didn't want its rankings involved in the process anymore. The AP's reasoning was sound: Staging an athletic competition based on a vote is ridiculous. The AP poll was created as a promotional tool designed to foster arguments. It was harmless fun. The BCS was not.

That left only the venerable coaches' poll, which rarely includes votes by the actual coaches. Overloaded with game preparation, recruiting, and bailing players out of the local jail, head coaches lack the time to watch teams around the country. Some can't be bothered to cast their own ballots. Those duties often fall to administrative assistants or media relations directors.

"I don't know why we vote," South Carolina coach Steve Spurrier said. "I guess we vote because college football is still without a playoff system. I really believe most coaches do not know a whole lot about the other teams."

Some votes are downright embarrassing. Missouri coach Gary Pinkel ranked a 12-0 Utah team 15th in the country at the end of 2008. Miles, the LSU coach, placed unbeaten Cincinnati eighth in the final ballot of 2009. The biases, whether big versus small, hewing to a region, or staying true to a conference, are blatant.

"I watched some of the voting patterns," former Kansas

coach Mark Mangino told the *Denver Post.* "I can see areas where guys weren't voting for teams they probably should have."

Before the 2009 season, coaches told the Cartel they would participate if their weekly votes were anonymous. As such, fans couldn't sniff out the side deals and alliances. A coach trying to secure a BCS championship game spot could move his team to No. 1 and leave competitors off the ballot. The BCS wouldn't allow it, and the coaches caved.

In the final 2009 poll, Cincinnati and Texas Christian were fighting for a long-shot chance they might sneak into the top two of the BCS standings. Cincinnati coach Brian Kelly voted his team No. 1 and TCU No. 4. TCU coach Gary Patterson ranked his team second and Cincinnati sixth. Imagine what they would've done had the Cartel not insisted their ballots be public. A secret ballot would forever kill the coaches' poll, and without that, the Cartel loses one of its best tools of collusion.

Another was born in 2005, after the AP withdrew. The BCS wanted a second human poll to balance the coaches' obvious prejudice. The more culprits, the better. Such was the impetus for the Harris Interactive College Football Poll, better known as the Harris Poll, a smorgasbord of people whose collective ignorance toward the current landscape of college football makes their voting even more foul than the coaches'.

While the media, coaches, and even coaches' secretaries aren't particularly adept at ranking teams, college football is the undeniable focus of their lives. Not so with Harris Poll voters, who aren't chosen by Harris Interactive or from some huge pool of applicants. Conferences nominate and sponsor voters, whose history of back-scratching is evident. While many Harris Poll voters are former players or administrators, they have families and businesses and other interests. Understandably, they follow the game only so much. That their previous involvement in football gives them sufficient expertise is like arguing that a long-retired Honda mechanic could service a 2010 BMW.

A few years ago, a *New York Times* reporter tracked down a Harris voter at a construction site. The interview began after the voter laid down his jackhammer. In the final 2008 poll, the only one that really matters, CBS announcer Don Criqui didn't even bother to send in his ballot. Among those Harris Poll voters who do turn in their rankings, fingerprints of favoritism appear everywhere. In 2009, Eric Mizell, a former Troy State player, gave his 25th-place vote to—guess who?—the same Troy team that had yielded fifty-six points in nonconference losses to Florida and Alabama. In a ballot that assisted Cincinnati, Mike McGee voted TCU eighth, behind two-loss teams from Ohio State, Penn State, and Oregon. McGee used to be Cincinnati's athletic director.

The bias is complemented by an ignorance that permeates the Harris Poll. In November 2008, *Daily Oklahoman* columnist Berry Tramel asked Pat Quinn, a retired Oklahoma State media relations director and Harris Poll voter, which team was on top of his ballot. The following exchange happened.

QUINN: Oh, I don't know. Doesn't really matter.

TRAMEL: Really?

QUINN: I think Alabama and Penn State will probably play for the national championship.

TRAMEL: You do?

QUINN: They're the only undefeated teams, aren't they?

TRAMEL: Uh, actually, Penn State had a loss.

QUINN: Oh, well. Those Big Ten teams have a lot of votes.

This is someone the Cartel thinks is uniquely qualified to help determine its title-game matchup.

The University of Utah actually did go undefeated in 2008 but was relegated to the Sugar Bowl because nearly every Harris Poll voter ranked the school between sixth and tenth. The groupthink is undeniable. Voters admit they consult other polls when filling out their ballot, and it makes completely baseless preseason predictions important—Death by *Athlon*, if you will.

The Mountain West Conference didn't have a major broadcast partner to do its bidding like the SEC or Big Ten does, and Utah's gaudy record provided no traction. Perception overwhelmed reality. Had Utah gone undefeated in the Pac-10, it probably would've played for the title. Instead, it ran the table in a league that had gone 6–1 against the Pac-10. By winning a better conference without the cachet, Utah was punished by voters who weren't paying attention.

When Utah manhandled Alabama in the Sugar Bowl to cap its 13-0 season, the college football world buzzed about the Utes' size and speed and skill, and how they would've presented a far greater challenge than Oklahoma to national champion Florida. The voters had whiffed on Utah, and it was fair to seek out a few Harris Poll members and ask whether they bothered to even watch the Utes before dismissing them as unworthy of competing for a national title.

"I did not see them play," Bobby Aillet said.

"I didn't see any live games," Lance McIlhenny said. "I just [saw] highlights."

"I don't recall if I saw them play specifically during the regular season," David Housel said. "I don't remember a specific game."

How long did it take to find those three blind voters? Three calls.

Fans of the biggest schools realized Utah, at the very least, deserved consideration for the title game. If voters aren't going to bother watching a 12-0 school—which had gone 12-0 four years earlier, too—nobody can defend the Harris Poll's credibility.

By offering no guidelines to voters, the BCS claims its formula comes about organically. That's a cop-out. Not requiring the voters to adhere to certain standards allows the Cartel to throw up its hands and say it had nothing to do with the results, even though it's aware the most uninformed voters will default to the biggest brand name with the most TV exposure.

It's how Texas was chosen overwhelmingly by the 2009 voters. Cincinnati went undefeated, and Jeff Sagarin, the dean of computer rankings, deemed its conference, the Big East, tougher than the Big 12. TCU and Boise State went undefeated, and while their strength of schedule wasn't top-notch, each had beaten a team better than the Longhorns' best foe, Nebraska. That's how the Cartel likes it: The chase for a championship is nothing more than a popularity contest.

Better that than deign to the Mountain West Conference's request for a men's basketball–style selection committee that would consist of a dozen educated voters with set criteria to consider and debate. A dozen uncompromised people with a clear objective beats 175 who can't seem to get out of their own way. Though the endgame seems obvious, the Cartel won't bend.

"The system is working well," BCS executive director Bill Hancock said.

Absolutely. Except for the bumbling Harris Poll, the bogus coaches' poll, and a corrupt computer system. Other than all three parts of the formula used to fulfill the BCS's sole purpose, it's just dandy.

13 The Superfan

As a reporter for *Buckeye Sports Bulletin*, a weekly newspaper dedicated to covering Ohio State sports, Steve Helwagen wrote stories about the football team year-round—features, tidbits, interviews, anything he could find, even in the dead of June. The *Bulletin* was a niche publication, desperate to reach Ohio State's vast alumni network. In 1997, a year before the BCS was born, it started posting stories on the Internet.

At the time, year-round media coverage of college football hardly existed. During the off-season, the local *Columbus Dispatch* wouldn't report on the Buckeyes for weeks. Unless something major happened, "there was nothing," Helwagen said. The sport was still rooted in its past as a seasonal pursuit. So when Helwagen told people what he did for a living, they usually looked at him sideways—even in football-mad Columbus.

Today, Helwagen is the managing editor of the online fan site Bucknuts.com, which draws nearly 200,000 unique users a month, more than 5,000 of whom pay $100 for a yearly subscription to get every last bit of news and gossip possible on their favorite team. Ohio State fever is a multimillion-dollar business. BuckeyeGrove.com, BuckeyeSports.com, and The-Ozone.net also take a piece of Ohio State's mega-audience, each site larded with minutiae and fan message boards that spin twenty-four hours a day, 365 days a year.

The Internet has bred a new sort of sports consumer: the Superfan, a plugged-in, often maniacal follower who devotes massive amounts of time and money to following a sport. College football claims millions of them. Superfans know more about the team and the sport than their ancestors ever could. They watch, read, interact, debate, and live it. They travel to more games, absorb every morsel of news, and obsess not simply over national signing day but over unofficial visits of high school sophomores.

Almost nothing is the same as it was before the Internet changed the game—except the system that governs college football's championship.

The Cartel congratulates itself for the spike in college football's popularity, which is the sporting equivalent of Al Gore taking credit for creating the Internet. The BCS wasn't an engine for college football's rise. It's an anchor with a broken reel. Twelve years ago, the Cartel formed the BCS to avoid one of its most pertinent problems: split national titles, such as the one Nebraska and Michigan shared in 1997. It hasn't even managed to do that: Louisiana State and Southern Cal were co-champions in 2003.

The BCS is woefully outdated, a dial-up connection in the broadband era. Businesses today modernize by the minute or die, and the Cartel has approved one significant change since its inception: adding a fifth BCS game. Perhaps no other consumer-driven industry has changed less in these adapt-or-vanish times. And the Cartel wonders why fans holler with such vitriol when the BCS goes bad.

Superfans beg for evolution. They want a playoff for the additional excitement, for the season that roars to a conclusion instead of stalling out and hoping it got things right. They want to see who's best, without any maybes attached. The amount and depth of coverage has grown exponentially in the last five years. An avalanche of information and the ability for fans to engage with each other on message boards, in chat rooms, and through Twitter feeds have launched interest in the sport to stratospheric levels, placing college football behind only the NFL in popularity.

Even the dinosaurs of print media recognized the need to change. More than a half-dozen Ohio newspapers now staff the team from January 1 to December 31. They rarely miss a day, even in the off-season, to give Ohio State fans their football fix. They blog. They tweet. They chat. Joining them are the two full-time sports talk radio stations in Columbus that go heavy on the Buckeyes.

Forget an off-season. On the hyper-focused Internet, there's no longer an off-afternoon. And it's not just Ohio State. College football is a massive product with a ravenous audience and providers happy to oblige. No one questions what Helwagen does for a living anymore.

"Now they ask about recruits," he said. "For fans, it's a borderline obsession. People build their year around following college football."

Consider the once-humble spring game, which used be an informal intrasquad scrimmage to offer players a light at the end of the off-season workout tunnel. Now it's an event, some televised locally and, thanks to ESPN, nationally. In 2007, 92,138 fans packed Bryant-Denny Stadium to witness Nick Saban's first Alabama spring game. *Sports Illustrated* featured it in a cover story. Not to be outdone, Ohio State set a new spring-practice attendance record in 2009 when 95,722 watched the Buckeyes in a practice game.

"When people make that kind of emotional and financial investment to being a fan of a particular college, they have an expectation that their school is going to be treated fairly," Helwagen said. "When it's not, that's a big problem."

Bigger than the Cartel realizes. The Superfan demands answers, the BCS offers excuses. The Cartel fiddles while the fans' anger burns.

In 2009, when the University of Cincinnati was en route to becoming just the second BCS conference team to go unbeaten and be shut out of the title game, the school's Superfans were enraged. They felt the system cheated their team, denied it an opportunity, said the Bearcats weren't worthy because their stadium was too small, or their team's history not illustrious enough, or some other feckless reason.

For decades, college fans were accustomed to occasional unbeaten seasons not meriting a No. 1 ranking. Now they can't tolerate such injustices. Joe Paterno had it happen to him four times at Penn State, including as recently as 1994. In 1968–69, Penn State had back-to-back 11–0 seasons and didn't win a title either time. Everyone shrugged and accepted the order of the bureaucracy, the limitations of the system. They complained in State College diners and bars. Fans today unload on the Internet.

To counter the Cincinnati uprising, the Cartel set up an appearance for executive director Bill Hancock on Dan Patrick's syndicated radio show, where Hancock said that as a consolation prize he'd give Bearcats coach Brian Kelly a hearty pat on the back and tell him, "You guys had a great season and you're to be congratulated for it."

It wasn't just Cincinnati fan message boards that almost collapsed in anger. Superfans across the country were outraged at Hancock's condescending and patronizing answer. He was mocking their team and, by proxy, their commitment. The fight between fans and the BCS isn't just a matchup of slow-witted executives and angry customers. It's a clash of cultures and generations, and it's one the Cartel will never win.

Each year, another group of young fans demanding modernization of the sport is born while a group that still believes in the value of backslaps and cherishes memories of the Bluebonnet Bowl fades away. The demographics will eventually topple the system.

"There's nothing like the Internet, and there never has been," said Bobby Burton, a former University of Texas football manager and recruiting newsletter editor who created the spawning ground of the Superfan when he purchased and rebranded Rivals.com in 2001. The leader of the modern fan-site industry was a late convert, not logging on to the Internet until 1997. That day at a friend's house, Burton experienced everything the Internet could be: addictive, fulfilling, and ripe for the sports fan.

"I went on at about 10:00 P.M. and I probably didn't get off until four in the morning," he said. "It kind of grabbed me immediately. I had no idea what it could turn into today, but I knew as a medium it is unmatched in many ways."

Less than four years later he was part of a partnership group that took over Rivals, then a bankrupt, post-Internet-bubble company featuring a ragtag string of Web sites attached to fan magazines—*Irish Illustrated* at Notre Dame, *Spartan Magazine* at Michigan State, *Tiger Illustrated* at Clemson. Knowing that endless information and a place to discuss it would attract readers, Rivals started individual sites for every major Division I-A school and encouraged them to focus on recruiting team news big and small, and, of course, message boards that would grow into massive communities. In 2007, Yahoo! bought the company for a reported $90 million.

"In the early days, people tried to compare the Internet to talk radio because they thought it was a bunch of mindless chatter," Burton said. "But the reality is the power of the community is so much more than talk radio could be. Talk radio talks at you. With the Internet, it's so much more about involvement on a personal level. The appetite is there. We just fed the hungry."

Soon everyone was trying to satisfy an insatiable fan base. Recruiting, previously newsworthy only on signing day, became an industry. Independent sites like Bucknuts.com sprung up across the Web. Nearly every major-conference program has between two and four sites dedicated to it. Blogs—from the wry Every Day Should Be Saturday to the hyper-local MGoBlog that covers Michigan—offered coverage at a depth never before contemplated.

Sports-talk radio exploded as a medium and moved from beyond the pro sports–dominated big cities to college towns. The Internet took low-watt, mom-and-pop stations and allowed them to stream around the globe. An expat in Istanbul could walk around Taksim Square listening to a podcast about Virginia Tech football on his iPhone, then pull up a browser and post his thoughts on a message board. No longer does it matter if you live in Blacksburg or by the Black Sea. Everything is available to readers who live in a campus dormitory or half a world away.

During the twentieth century, college football was a regional pursuit. The ultimate goal for Woody Hayes and Bo Schembechler was to go to the Rose Bowl. Winning it was a secondary pursuit. In twenty seasons at Michigan, Schembechler never captured a national title or completed a perfect season, yet his ability to win or share thirteen Big Ten championships made him an infallible legend. His 5-12 bowl record was ignored.

At Ohio State, Hayes went 2-6 in his final eight bowl appearances and "nobody cared," Helwagen said. "It was, 'My God, the man is a legend.'" Current coach Jim Tressel is 8-1 against

Michigan, has won five consecutive Big Ten championships, and reached five consecutive BCS bowl games. When the Buckeyes lost three of them in a row, "there [was] an undercurrent of disillusion," Helwagen said. "Now they've seen there is something out there, a brighter star to reach for. And when you don't get it, they're upset. They don't understand."

Pre-Internet, the idea of a split national title was frustrating but at least passable. Though the two national opinion polls—the AP and the coaches—might choose different teams as champions, each school could hold a parade and pretend the other didn't exist. If there was a geographical separation—Miami, Florida, is closer to Bolivia than to the University of Washington, with which it split the 1991 title—fan interaction was minimal.

The Internet has made the world smaller, and no matter how segmented the college football universe, it's ultimately woven like wicker. Everyone has access to everyone else. Used to be that like-minded fans could comfort one another in break rooms at work or dorm lounges after a loss. Rival fans today don't bother waiting until the game is over to commence the trash talk. The ability to heckle takes one click and a few keystrokes.

The Superfans' relentlessness caused a shift in expectations and drove college football's supersizing: bigger coaching salaries, better facilities, and larger conferences, all to help chase the influx of money. Tradition means nothing in the pursuit of money to feed the beast. Coaches have tried to match the intensity, meet the demands of the job, and now only the strongest and most committed survive. The dadgum days of Bobby Bowden, who retired from Florida State in 2009, have given way to a generation of workaholic robo-coaches such as Florida's Urban Meyer. Nothing is the same in the post-Internet world, and no one should bother claiming as much.

Except the Cartel tries. Rather than understanding and accommodating the growing ranks of Superfans, they've chosen to paint them as crazies, dismiss them as unimportant, or plain ignore their passion.

Hancock, the exceedingly polite but saccharine spokesman for the BCS, still believes fans will accept the BCS's failures as an agree-to-disagree fact of life. Instead, he has become the face of the Cartel's misguided social-media campaign, routinely ridiculed by fans for his illogical, aw-shucks radio interviews and the BCS's mind-numbing Twitter posts that don't seem to understand the basic tenets of modern retail. As *Advertising Age* lectured the BCS: "If you know your product is universally loathed, Twitter is not the place for you."

The third post of the official BCS Twitter feed, @INSIDE theBCS, cited a quote from Meyer calling the BCS "not perfect, but it has been great for college football." Hancock forgot to point out that when Meyer coached Utah, he told the *New York Times*: "The system is a failure."

Fans raged against the Twitter feed and its equally ridiculous Web companion, PlayoffProblem.com. One Twitter user signed up for an account, typed out a one-line blast—*@geemann2236: @INSIDEtheBCS We hate you. Signed, Everyone. Thank you.*—and never posted again. Hundreds of comments trashing the BCS littered its anti-playoff Web site on which it tried to argue with opponents. It could be called propaganda, but propaganda actually works.

When a ten-minute radio interview produces countless message board threads, not to mention wall-to-wall calls on talk shows around the country, it's not the sign of a branding snafu. It's a problem that runs to the core of the product.

"The fans are more educated," Burton said. "The more personally you buy in to the game, the more you read, the more you follow it, the deeper you get into something and the more personal involvement you have. Then when the BCS is screwing with your team, it is screwing with you."

The Cartel asks generations of fans obsessed with near-daily advancement in their world to support the ineffective, old way. The Cartel tells consumers who have wrested control that they might as well go along with the current structure because some faceless men sitting in an ivory tower say so. The Cartel wants the people who spend their paychecks and devote their time to be satisfied with an old-fashioned congratulatory slap on the back for the 12-0 regular season that, for whatever reason, just isn't good enough.

And when it realizes none of that works, the Cartel will find itself confronted by a great lesson of the Internet age: The product always bows to the masses, not the other way around.

14 All in a *GameDay*'s Work

If college football is a religion, then its weekly service is a two-hour, nationally televised revival featuring four preachers and a swarming mass of worshippers who hang on every word when they're not too busy draining a beer from their tailgate.

Each Saturday morning at 10:00 ET, outside a frenzied stadium, ESPN's *College GameDay* pregame show reminds college football's flock of all that is sacred and worthwhile about the sport. This is the Superfan's spiritual nourishment, a program that counts millions of viewers nationwide, thousands on-set, and, perhaps, one from high above. In 2000, *GameDay* analyst Lee Corso picked Georgia Tech to defeat Virginia Tech at Lane Stadium, the Hokies' home field. Moments later, a lightning bolt singed his rental car. "I don't know what a Hokie is," Corso said, "but God is one of 'em."

Amid the divinity stands a false idol. The Cartel likes to claim the growth of college football over the past decade is directly due to the BCS. God knows, as does any Hokie, Bruin, Aggie, Razorback, Panther, or Badger, that television is as responsible as anything. Whether it's the pageantry of *GameDay* or the expansion of coverage to provide noon-to-night action on Saturday and games almost every day of the week, TV helped college football evolve into a behemoth—one that outgrew the BCS long ago.

GameDay pushed televised college football coverage beyond the on-field action and took fans on a coast-to-coast carnival ride. It didn't just show games. It showcased the sport: the culture, the tradition, the passion, and the fun—one campus, one mascot head, one debate at a time.

Saturday morning used to be for cartoons. Now, an entire generation has grown up watching *GameDay,* and the television's impact on college football's evolution is direct and tangible. A regional pastime morphed into a national frenzy. Recruiting boundaries faded. Respect and recognition no longer tied themselves to history and location. Anger bubbled over a paternalistic championship system in which the Cartel claimed to know what and who is best. The Internet and television grew in tandem, played off each other, and created a groundswell the Cartel can't stop.

"No question it's a different sport," said John Wildhack, ESPN's vice president for programming, who worked on *GameDay* in the early 1990s. "It's far more popular, it's bigger, it's better, and the depth is remarkable, compared to where it was fifteen, twenty years ago. In the mid-1990s, there may have been eight to ten blue-chip programs. Now you can go thirty, thirty-five teams deep."

Which doesn't exactly benefit a system that haphazardly selects two teams and deems them the best. Life would be so much easier for the Cartel had the *GameDay* crew not figured out how to go beyond the highlights and connect with the sport's lifeblood.

Back in 1993, *GameDay* was a quality studio show, driven by the chemistry of host Chris Fowler serving as referee between the strong, educated opinions of a former coach, Corso, and a former player, Craig James. It lacked the ability to channel college football's excitement. Three guys wearing suits in a Connecticut studio never could convey the pre-kickoff energy of Clemson's Death Valley or the color of the Volunteer Navy on the Tennessee River or the beauty of the Flatirons above Folsom Field in Boulder, Colorado. As anyone who has attended a college game knows, only half the action occurs on the field.

When No. 1 Florida State and No. 2 Notre Dame were on a collision course for a November 1993 showdown, ESPN wondered about dropping *GameDay* down by Touchdown Jesus. The enthusiasm of a South Bend Saturday could seep into the broadcast, transporting new viewers along with it. There were logistical risks, of course. This was live TV. Soon enough, everyone agreed it was worth the gamble, and by 1994, ESPN no longer could confine *GameDay* to a studio.

Sixteen years later, the show is a traveling extravaganza, complete with its own RV, an on-site crew seventy-five strong, screaming minions in every city, and a quartet of hosts who are treated like rock stars: Fowler, Corso, Kirk Herbstreit, and Desmond Howard need a security detail to get to and from the set. Their cell phones blow up with coaches begging them to bring the show to their campus for what's considered a two-hour recruiting infomercial and the ultimate stamp of legitimacy.

GameDay anchors ESPN's concept of turning each week of the season into episodic TV, an amalgam of action, drama, and suspense. The Superfan gets up in the morning with word on the possible plot developments and can stay until midnight for *College Football Final*, a lively in-studio recap featuring host Rece Davis and analysts Mark May and Lou Holtz. The day turns into an experience, a chance to live vicariously through fans who migrate from a party-filled quad to the *GameDay* set to the stadium and back home to soak in another game or two.

Campuses come alive when *GameDay* arrives. In 1996, Corso began donning a mascot head to signify his final prediction for

the on-site game, and he finds himself the most popular or vilified man in town every week depending on which he chooses.
Superfans wake up at 6:00 A.M. to stake out a spot so they can
cheer or boo Corso's choice of mascot head. When 30,000 purple-
clad Kansas State fans showed up in 1998, ESPN moved the show
inside the stadium to accommodate them. With cameras trained
on the crowds, signs both colorful and off-color began sprouting
up, one-upmanship always encouraged.

It's such an event that fans of teams not even playing in that
day's game show up. In 2003, a Washington State alum named
Tom Pounds drove eight hundred miles from his home in Albu-
querque, New Mexico, to fly a dark red Cougars flag among the
crowd in Austin, Texas. Two weeks later, he shipped "Ol' Crimson" to another Wazzu alum who drove to a *GameDay* broadcast
in Madison, Wisconsin. It got forwarded to Ohio, then Oklahoma, and on and on. There hasn't been a *GameDay* since without either Ol' Crimson or its companion, "Ol' White"—and
sometimes both—flying in the background, a streak expected
to break one hundred games in 2010.

"If we were doing this for the NBA or the NFL or even college
basketball, it wouldn't have the same feel," said Herbstreit, the
former Ohio State quarterback who replaced James in 1996 just
as the show began heading out weekly. "In college football, the
fan bases are so passionate and authentic. That's the difference.
We don't tell them, 'OK, now you cheer.' There is no applause
sign. We're in the middle of a tailgate on these college campuses,
and we just have to turn the camera on amidst all these [meat]
smokers and tailgates and people. It's like, 'OK, let's set up there.'
And it's all around us."

So whether it's windy, rainy, snowy, freezing, scorching, or
humid, *GameDay* shows up. It doesn't discriminate where, either.
The crew has traveled to an Ivy League game, another between

historically black colleges, the Division III Amherst-Williams rivalry, and all three service academies. With *GameDay* familiarizing places big and small, nowhere is too far away, no coach too obscure, no campus town anonymous. The college football world shrinks by the year.

When forming the BCS, the Cartel knew it could get away with telling the fans which teams were and weren't worthy of championship consideration. There were often fewer than ten games on TV a week, forcing fans to trust panels of sportswriters or coaches or computers. Now the games are wall-to-wall, two to three dozen a week on ESPN's various platforms alone. Then there's CBS, NBC, Versus, and Fox Sports regional outlets. The Big Ten created its own television network, in part to assure its lesser teams airtime. You can pretty much watch anyone, any week.

In the 1990s, fans in the Midwest might tune in to the Rose Bowl to see what kind of team USC had. Now they've watched eight or nine Trojans games live. Anyone can scout a smaller-conference school and believe in their ability or dismiss their credentials. The opinion is self-generated, unfiltered, a direct descendant of *GameDay*'s democratic view.

"ESPN's commentators have given credibility to programs such as Utah, TCU, and Boise State," Western Athletic Conference commissioner Karl Benson said.

Of course, despite how big *GameDay* and the Internet have made college football, the TV ratings for some of the biggest postseason games remain mediocre, a direct indictment of the one-off nature of the bowl system and the inability of the BCS to deliver the compelling matchups it idly promises. Aside from the title game and the Rose Bowl, which benefits from a 5:00 P.M. ET time slot on New Year's Day, college football games rarely are broadcast ratings hits.

The 2010 Orange Bowl did a pedestrian 6.8 rating and got pilloried by *NCIS,* its stepbrother *NCIS: Los Angeles,* and a rookie show, *The Good Wife.* In 2010, the NFL's four wild card games, despite disadvantageous time slots—weekend afternoons rather than Thursday primetime—averaged a higher rating than the BCS title game (18.1 to 17.2). In the divisional round, the ratings leapt into the 20s, with the Dallas Cowboys–Minnesota Vikings game posting a 23.9 despite starting early Sunday afternoon. The conference-championship round spiked into the 30s. It's not just the NFL's popularity. Playoffs, with their eminently more important games, come with the requisite intrigue to draw diehards and casual fans alike.

The month-or-so layoff between the end of the regular season and the BCS bowls slays any momentum from conference championship games, and the one-and-done structure of the BCS prevents an exciting game from carrying over. The last Rose Bowl played to an audience no doubt enthralled by the play of Ohio State quarterback Terrelle Pryor. Rather than tune in the following week and see more, Pryor converts would have to wait nine months. In the NCAA basketball tournament, obscure players, such as Davidson's Stephen Curry in 2008, can become overnight stars and singular reasons to watch.

The event can take on a life of its own. In 2010, low-profile Butler, a small private school from Indianapolis, reached the men's national title game against Duke. Rather than hurt the ratings, the game produced the most viewers since 1997, according to CBS. The audience was up 31 percent over the 2009 title game between name opponents North Carolina and Michigan State. That's the power of a dream-big one-and-done tournament.

Considering the endless press releases touting television ratings "success," the Cartel's standards are low. College football's ratings are strong only when compared to the past.

Though no American sport matches the NFL in terms of fan interest, college football lags proportionally further behind pro football than college basketball does behind the NBA. Today's college football ratings are Lilliputian next to those potentially drawn by playoff matchups culminating in a true national-championship game.

A playoff, current and former television executives said, would be an enormous success because it is an interconnected series of events that plays so well to mega-corporations versed in promotion across different mediums. Football, even more than basketball, is perfectly built to capture the fair-weather audience. The week off between games allows for backstories to be told, predictions to be made, and casual fans to catch up on what they missed.

"The snowball momentum of a playoff would build to a crescendo of interest that's never been seen in college football," said Ben Goss, an associate professor of sports marketing at Missouri State. "The ratings would follow."

Estimated one current sports television executive: "The semifinals would do what the current title game does, high teens. The championship game, at that point, is a big-time television event, mid-20s at least."

ESPN has done its part to grow not just ratings but the entire sport, something of limited interest to the BCS. Taking *GameDay* on the road is an expensive production, and ESPN executives admit they could turn a greater profit by returning the show to the studio, even if the ratings dipped. They know better than to risk ruining a franchise by chasing a few dollars.

College football is too important to the network. For years, the SEC had near-exclusive rights to ESPN's Saturday prime-time slot, a crown jewel of promotion. There was perhaps no better way to sell Southern football than in packed stadiums under the lights on national TV. When ESPN expanded its Saturday-night offerings to showcase non-SEC games on ABC and ESPN2, Mike Slive, the SEC commissioner, was furious. He called ESPN's home base in Bristol, Connecticut, and, as he put it, began "ranting and raving."

"[It] appeared to me to be intuitively a competitive situation and not necessarily good for us," Slive said. "And they said to me, 'Your ratings will go up.' And I said, 'No way.'"

ESPN was right. By counterprogramming college football with even more college football, everyone's ratings went up, even the conference that used to have a monopoly on the time slot.

"We did a lot of research," said Wildhack, the ESPN executive. "The average fan watches forty minutes of a three-hour game. So the diehard fan is watching all three hours of their team, but there are a lot of people that are surfing in and out of games. So if we can navigate that audience by updating what's happening in other games, we can move them between our networks. Giving them as much choice as possible, there seems to be an insatiable appetite for college football in this country."

And no conference better illustrates that than the SEC, which has maximized the power of television. Over the last twenty years, the conference left behind its local roots and expanded like a big-box franchise. Everyone knows the SEC, and it's hard not to appreciate a conference that has won four straight national championships. CBS and ESPN paid a combine $3 billion to televise SEC games for fifteen years.

In 2009, CBS's national broadcast of the SEC game of the week actually drew larger audiences than ABC's regional broadcasts of other conferences, which showed local teams in their home markets. The SEC was beating other leagues in their own backyards. It is almost NFL Lite, its coaches and players outsize

personalities, its controversies full of staying power and reso-
nance. You didn't need to live in the South to have an opinion
about Tim Tebow, who was the story of the 2010 NFL Draft
even as he went to Denver with the 25th overall pick.

"We have become a national brand," Slive said.

The expansion of television—and the information delivered
by *GameDay* and ESPN's other shows—has likewise changed
the recruiting game. Top players consider schools beyond the
brand-name programs because they can see the offense and defense and get a sense of the crowd and hear the fight song from
thousands of miles away. No longer do players resist attending
a school two time zones from their homes. And the talent has
leveled out accordingly.

"It's no longer a regional sport," Herbstreit said. "It's become a national deal where everyone is dialed in. You have to
be dialed in to every game. Because of that I think the popularity is greater than it ever has been."

Herbstreit owns a front-row seat to the hysteria, and he
need only turn around and see the zoo behind him. *GameDay*'s
ratings are bigger, its crowds bolder. Week after week, the show
connects a nation of fans to the pulse of college football. More
hype. More parity. More anticipation.

College football is a made-for-TV mega-power, and ESPN
understands it's the perfect conduit through which the sport
can proselytize to the masses. The BCS doesn't. The current
system captures none of the emotion, the hope, the possibility,
the atmosphere. It's not an event. It's not something that excites
people. It's a cold, calculating, governing bureaucracy, the tax
man of sports.

It's black and white in a pastime whose growth is perhaps best
personified by a bright primary color in the unlikeliest of places.

15 Blue Turf vs. Blue Blood

Gene Bleymaier was thirty-two when divine inspiration struck, quite literally, out of the blue. Because he had already been the athletic director at Boise State University for four years, he didn't flinch at walking into the school president's office with his biggest, boldest, craziest idea yet, perfect for the upstart program he was building in Idaho's capital.

Blue turf.

It was a forward-thinking, big-dreaming concept that symbolizes one of the BCS's problems: The rise of the nobody. When the Cartel designed the BCS in the mid-1990s, such small-conference programs as Boise State, Texas Christian, Utah, Houston, and Fresno State might as well have not existed. The Cartel built the BCS on an outdated model of college football's power structure. It deemed members of the six major conferences legitimate and everyone else not. Even among those conferences, there was a clear delineation between the elite and unworthy. The premise was borne of the Cartel's never-ending paternalism: It knows who plays real football and who doesn't, and any team that succeeds outside the power structure deserves a nice little pinch on its cute cheek.

And then along came Boise State.

It started with Bleymaier's crazy idea, one not even he could possibly have seen as the harbinger of an anonymous, out-of-the-way program crashing two Fiesta Bowls and winning both. The school's modest Bronco Stadium playing surface was green back then, just like everyone else's. That was the problem, Bleymaier figured. If you've got a I-AA football program, in Idaho no less, with aspirations of grandeur, you can't afford to be just like everyone else. If you wait around for the rest of the country to notice you, it won't.

Bleymaier thought he had a sleeping giant in Boise. The school was growing fast. Two decades earlier, it had been a junior college. The city was Idaho's largest—beautiful and surprisingly cosmopolitan—and the metropolitan population of a quarter million would more than double over the next twenty years. This wasn't some tiny, cornfield-surrounded college town. Locals were desperate for a sports program to support. There were Fortune 500 companies to tap.

He just needed a hook, something to make people locally, regionally, and nationally not only notice Boise State but remember it. The green turf was old, so Bleymaier found a company that would install the new carpet for $750,000, regardless of color.

"The idea came to me that there is no reason why the field is green," Bleymaier said. "We're not fooling anyone. They know it's not grass. So why should it be green? Why not make it our school colors? When you go to Lincoln, Nebraska, everything is red but the field. When you go to Knoxville, Tennessee, everything is orange but the field. So we said, 'Hey, come to Boise and you'll see blue.'"

Boise State president John Keiser was convinced, except for one hitch: He worried the blue turf would be an aesthetic disaster. While the company could do blue, it had never deviated from green. It couldn't even offer a picture of what the field might look like. Bleymaier improvised, turning the tint on his old TV toward blue and creating a reasonable facsimile.

Boise State took the plunge in 1986, and the turf was a hit. Fans loved it. Players, too. The program moved to Division I-A in 1996, its Smurf Turf already a cult legend. Travelers along I-84 often stopped to take pictures of the turf around which apocryphal stories blossomed. One said before the lines and logos were painted on the field, birds and ducks mistook the turf for a pond, which they dive-bombed to their ultimate demise. Bleymaier, ever the promoter, always understanding the value of publicity—even in the form of crazy lore that might retroactively offend PETA—keeps the legend alive with his hemming and hawing.

"I can neither confirm nor deny that report," he said, laughing. "That's my story and I'm sticking to it."

Faraway television executives were intrigued by the gimmick and soon found when they threw the blue turf on television, remote controls stopped mid-click. Maybe it was out of curiosity, but fans stayed and watched.

Soon it wasn't just the field that made them dizzy. Boise State went for it on fourth-and-long, saw two-point conversions as an opportunity, and regularly spread the field with five wide receivers. In the late 1990s, few took Boise State seriously, but damn if they weren't fun to watch. People did, and the high ratings meant more TV games. The Broncos played on weeknights, late nights—basically anytime ESPN asked, figuring a scheduling inconvenience here and there would pay dividends in recruiting.

"People who were progressive thinkers saw the advantage of weeknight games," said John Wildhack, ESPN's vice president of programming. "We've got a philosophy at ESPN: Any team can play their way on. Boise hasn't only played their way on, they've stayed on."

In 2009, the Broncos played eight times in nationally televised games, making them one of the most visible teams in the country. They also won more games in the 2000s than any other team—with five undefeated regular seasons—captured seven of the last eight Western Athletic Conference championships, and, over that span, posted a 55-1 conference record.

The program's moment of glory came in the 2007 Fiesta Bowl, when ultra-underdog Boise State beat storied Oklahoma on a series of late-game trick plays called by never-rattled coach Chris Petersen. The final score came on a daring two-point conversion in overtime courtesy of a Statue of Liberty play to running back Ian Johnson.

Minutes later, with Fox's Chris Myers calling the play-by-play, Johnson proposed to his cheerleader girlfriend, Chrissy Popadics, on national television. She said yes.

You couldn't make this stuff up.

The game is considered one of the most famous and exciting in college football history, and it quickly became a recurring nightmare for the Cartel. Boise State had the nation buzzing, and its performance begged for a playoff. The Broncos were 13-0, the only undefeated team in the nation. Football fans pined to see what else Petersen kept in his book of magic tricks. The rest of the country wanted to know more about Johnson and his cheerleader fiancée. *Good Morning America*, *Entertainment Tonight*, and *People* magazine called. Hollywood agents wanted to pitch the couple on TV shows and movie scripts. Almost everybody agreed: These giant killers deserved another game.

Americans are trained to watch sports through the prism of a playoff. Win and keep playing. When George Mason, a commuter school in suburban Washington, D.C., upset powerhouse Michigan State in the opening round of the 2006 NCAA men's basketball tournament, it didn't congratulate itself and call it a season. Everyone got to watch as the Patriots took on mighty

North Carolina two nights later. They won again. Two games later, they beat Connecticut to advance to the Final Four. By then, George Mason was the nation's darling, only to be supplanted four years later by Butler.

It took the same amount of time for Boise State to follow up its Fiesta Bowl triumph with something of equal import. The milestone win over Oklahoma so shifted the paradigm of college football that when the Broncos returned to the Fiesta Bowl in 2010, fans were irate. Rather than face Texas Christian, the Mountain West's undefeated entry, Boise State wanted to overwhelm another big-conference opponent. The game was dubbed the "Separate but Equal Bowl" by *Sports Illustrated's* Andy Staples. Rep. Jim Matheson (D-Utah) went one step further: "The Kids' Table Bowl."

Boise State had gone from not being good enough for a BCS game to a BCS game not being good enough for Boise State. Blue turf was turning blue blood.

For the Cartel, Boise's success wasn't something to celebrate. The BCS's exclusionary practices work only if it can convince the public that teams from non–big six conferences are so weak and lowly that their gaudy, unbeaten records are specters. The Cartel's best way to suppress demand for fair bowl access or a full-on playoff is through a campaign of disrespect, a case that thins by the day.

"They really do look down on Hawaii or Utah," a current television executive said. "They don't want to be on the same field as them. In the same vicinity."

The Cartel wants fans to believe that any non–big six conference team that happens to achieve a modicum of success is simply a shooting star that ought be ignored. It prefers the one-year glory of the Ball State Cardinals, a long-suffering program that streaked to a 12-0 regular-season record in 2008, threatened to

sneak into the BCS, and reverted the next year with seven consecutive losses to open the season. Ball State was a nice story and
no real threat on the national stage. Such flukes happen.

The Boise States of the world are different. They keep building and getting better. In 2011, they'll leave behind the WAC
for the more competitive Mountain West. It's no different than
Utah, the original BCS buster in 2005. It went 12-0 that year and
beat Big East champion Pittsburgh in the Fiesta Bowl behind
coach Urban Meyer. When Meyer left for Florida, everyone figured the Utes would go away. The school hired another dynamic
coach, Kyle Whittingham, who just four seasons later had put
together an even better Utah team that went 13-0 in 2008 and
beat Alabama 31–17 in the Sugar Bowl, part of its current nine–
bowl game winning streak. In the ultimate sign of respect, the
Utes will join the privileged Pac-10 in 2011, the outcast bullying
its way into the in crowd.

Meanwhile, Brigham Young, a storied program with a national title and a Heisman Trophy winner, hired Bronco Mendenhall and saw its program return to prominence. Down at
Texas Christian, coach Gary Patterson began fully mining the
talent-rich Metroplex region and churned out 10-win season
after 10-win season. Turns out the Horned Frogs were more
than just LaDainian Tomlinson.

In 2008, TCU produced more NFL Draft selections than any
other program in the state of Texas—more than Texas, Texas
Tech, or Texas A&M. Not that it mattered to Patterson, who
returned such tremendous talent that TCU finished the 2009
regular season 12-0 and made its first BCS bowl. The Horned
Frogs are no upstart.

These are programs. The schools poured money into practice facilities and stadium expansions. They upped recruiting
budgets and marketing. They kept improving. Meyer, even after

getting to Florida, said a school such as Utah has far more built-in advantages, including quality of city, than some BCS-level universities in smaller states or tiny towns.

"When we're able to get kids to visit, we have a very high success rate to get kids to commit," Whittingham said. "That's the key for us. Get recognized, get exposure, and get kids willing to come and take a look. We can recruit speed and athleticism here."

Utah's 13-0 season in 2008 was powered by skill-position players who all came from either California or Texas. All were African-Americans starring at the flagship university in a state that's nearly 93 percent white. That's college football today.

If Boise State relied on Idaho talent alone, it never would have left I-AA. In 2009, players hailed from all over the West, including thirty-five from California. The Broncos' best cornerback, NFL first-round pick Kyle Wilson, was from Piscataway, N.J. Like Whittingham, Petersen believes if he can get a kid to visit Boise, he can get him to commit. And the Broncos' near-decade-long dominance—they've managed the second-most BCS bowl appearances among West Coast teams despite their conference affiliation—reinforces that a talent diaspora indeed exists.

The explosion in media coverage means recruits in California, Florida, and Texas no longer tolerate waiting for playing time behind established upperclassmen at brand-name schools. Not only does ESPN beam in games from all over the country, the Internet provides extensive national media coverage and the ability for players to easily research and follow distant teams. Kids don't need to take an unofficial visit with Dad to see a school's weight room. There's a video tour on its Web site.

On YouTube, kids market themselves with highlight videos they hope pique the interest of a coach who otherwise may not have scouted them. One more click takes a player to Facebook,

MySpace, Twitter, and any number of social-networking sites that allow young prospects to keep in touch. In the '90s, top high school players may have attended a local summer camp where they would befriend other stars from the area and, quite often, plot their college choices together. Now, with regional talent camps run by Rivals.com, Reebok, and others, a quarterback from Orlando is friends with a lineman from Minnesota, and they text each other about playing together in Virginia.

"When I was in high school, I lived in the southeastern part of Ohio," said ESPN's Kirk Herbstreit, a highly recruited quarterback from suburban Dayton in 1988 who chose Ohio State. "You barely knew anything about the northeast part of the state. . . . No school is far away anymore."

In 2010, five of the top six prospects in Ohio left the state, including the top four as rated by Rivals.com. Ohio State, long a monopolist in Buckeye State recruiting, felt firsthand the sting of the modern game. The flow of talent elsewhere isn't stopping. Even the top players aren't averse to spurning traditional schools, and second-tier kids actively seek playing time no matter the locale.

Consider the state of Oregon, a mostly rural place with fewer than four million residents. It's best known for producing long-distance runners, not football players. Nike, the state's ubiquitous company, was created when the founders, including Phil Knight, made running shoe soles in waffle irons. They didn't know anything about football.

Historically, Oregon and Oregon State have been nonfactors in the Pac-10 title chase. Without a strong local talent base, they could never compete with USC, UCLA, or Washington. For years, college recruiting was a numbers game. Now they do it the way Boise has, getting what they can from their home area and recruiting relentlessly in other ZIP codes. Oregon and Oregon State took the ethos of the Internet and modern-day TV—boundaries no longer exist—and applied it to their recruiting efforts. The jersey may say Oregon, but the roster says something else. The schools draw out-of-state athletes with superior facilities, coaches, support, and way of life. There's a reason USC lost a game in the state of Oregon each season from 2006 to 2009.

At the end of the 2009 season, Oregon and Oregon State played their annual Civil War game, this time for the Pac-10 title. Oregon won thanks to huge performances from running backs LaMichael James (hometown: Texarkana, Texas) and LeGarrette Blount (Perry, Florida), quarterback Jeremiah Masoli (Daly City, California), and wide receiver Jeff Maehl (Paradise, California). That was enough to offset the brilliant play of Oregon State running back Jacquizz Rodgers (Richmond, Texas), quarterback Sean Canfield (Carlsbad, California), and linebacker Keaton Kristick (Fountain Hills, Arizona).

"That's how it's changed," Herbstreit said. "Two running backs from Texas, in a high-profile game, between two teams in Oregon that fringe fans would say, 'Who, what?' The fans don't know who the coaches are. The high school players, however, now know everything about these schools."

No matter how hard it tries, the Cartel no longer can brush off programs from the fringes of the power conferences or the top of the non–big six leagues. Fans don't just know Boise State is good, they know the ins and outs of the team. The names, faces, jerseys, and turf are recognizable and commoditized. Boise State, which now battles Oregon for recruits, beat the Ducks in the 2009 season's first week. The victory looked better as the season went on, and Boise State cracked the top 5 in November.

TCU eventually climbed to No. 3 thanks to a perfect season that featured victories over two ACC teams as well as Utah and BYU. Perhaps most telling was the unanimity with which the fans and media treated the Horned Frogs' success. They were legitimate, embraced even by the habitually misguided Harris Poll voters who a year earlier admitted they never bothered to watch Utah play. The Utes' victory against Alabama, coupled with Boise State's first Fiesta Bowl win, swayed the pendulum enough to change the discussion. No longer was it about how good the small-conference team could be. Now it was why that team wasn't getting the fair and equitable shot at a championship it deserved.

After TCU beat Utah in November 2009, *Sports Illustrated*'s Stewart Mandel wrote: "As I read through e-mails and scrolled through Twitter comments late Saturday from fans who were watching TCU—many of them for the first time—a common theme emerged:

"Wow . . . TCU is for real . . . Very impressed . . . as good as the 'top three' . . . deserve to play for national title.

"This is college football in 2009," Mandel wrote. "In the past, any mention of TCU (or Utah, or Boise State) in the same sentence as 'national title' would have immediately garnered smirks and the automatic response of 'Who have they played?' Now, there's an unquestioned respect level."

The fans have seen too many teams the Cartel claims are unworthy prove otherwise. Let the BCS live in its 1990s cocoon, where it discounts a team based on conference affiliation and home-state population or location. The fans know better. They know that college football, with burgeoning dynasties at Boise State and Utah and TCU, is better than it used to be.

It's as clear as the blue turf.

16 The Civil War

The Cartel absorbs attacks on a daily basis from, among others, fans, radio hosts, newspaper columnists, congressmen, and coaches. Out of the public view, it must fend off another threat, one far more acute and capable of breaking up the whole racket: itself.

Don't let its outward solidarity fool you. The BCS today is Hatfield vs. Hatfield, a system in a constant state of civil war, assaulted from within by feuding factions from conferences whose motivations dovetail less and less, according to a number of sources familiar with the strife. The BCS exists because the men in power didn't want to lose their conferences' stranglehold on money and influence, and as the landscape of college football shifts, so do their motivations.

Conferences are built to compete against each other, not cooperate and sing "Kumbaya." There are egos, rivalries, and backstabbing. Commissioners have no misgivings about playing wild-game hunter and poaching schools from other conferences. They squeeze every dollar, even if it endangers their so-called partners. Their opposition to changing the BCS is as much a product of self-serving inaction as anything. Truth is, while the Cartel defends the BCS, almost no one is satisfied with its current incarnation.

Mike Slive, the commissioner of the SEC, is among the

brightest and most well-regarded athletic administrators in the country. A onetime district court judge in New Hampshire, Slive was stung by the 2004 season when the BCS left his conference's unbeaten champion, Auburn, out of the title game. He decided to advocate a fairer plan for college football. "If you love the game, the goal is to help the game, not hurt the game," he said.

He and his staff spent two years crafting a comprehensive plan for a modest four-team playoff, also known as the plus-one because it would require only one additional game. Rather than endorsing a complete overhaul, he suggested a tweak that would leave the bowl system intact and generate another boatload of money for college football.

This was no big-dreaming fan with a wild plan. This was no Conference USA president claiming his team deserved a shot. This was the man in the middle of the Cartel, the head of the supercharged SEC. He certainly couldn't be accused of self-interest. At the time SEC teams were 4-0 in BCS title games and had won consecutive championships. Despite the Auburn disaster, if anyone was benefiting from the system, it was Mike Slive.

He came with the support of a number of his own university presidents, including Bernie Machen of the University of Florida and Michael Adams of the University of Georgia. ACC commissioner John Swofford and a number of that league's presidents, including Florida State's T. K. Wetherell, were also on board.

In the spring of 2008, Slive took his idea to the annual BCS meetings in Florida and laid it out to the other ten conference commissioners and the athletic director of Notre Dame.

Within a matter of hours, his proposal was dead. Slive's supposed Cartel allies—commissioners from the Big East, Big Ten, Big 12, and Pac-10—blocked its path. It didn't come up for a vote, in part because "we never vote," as one commissioner said. Five people in the room willing to make an estimate say it would have passed 8–4. The four big conferences that opposed the plan refused to even take it back to their respective presidents for discussion. Their stated fear: The plus-one might prove too popular and too profitable and ultimately expand into an eight- or sixteen-team playoff.

"We felt like there could be . . . more pressure to add more teams with an ability to get to the national championship game," Big 12 commissioner Dan Beebe said.

Perhaps this was comeuppance for fourteen years earlier, when Vince Dooley walked into the SEC meetings hoping to affect change and the conference brass put up an obstructionist barricade. With Slive, the Cartel hadn't merely snuffed out one of its own. It rebuked him in public for daring to step out of line. The ruling majority deemed something on which Slive had worked for two years unworthy of even a debate. When the SEC went on to win BCS championship games in 2009 and 2010 and ran its streak to four straight, conference staffers enjoyed a chuckle.

"This is a marathon and not a sprint," Slive said. There would be more fights to come, more dissatisfaction seeding itself throughout the system. The Cartel loves a good brawl. Unlike so many other fights it wages, this one didn't cost a penny.

The BCS hired two men in 2009 to shield itself from the grenades lobbed its way daily. One of them, executive director Bill Hancock, argued against a playoff by wondering how the cheerleaders and band members would handle it. The other, Ari Fleischer, orchestrated a public-relations campaign that went over like New Coke. The BCS does its best work surreptitiously, aiming to stave off congressional intervention and keep its stranglehold alive with an old quarterback who tries to navigate Washington, D.C., as well as he did the wishbone offense.

When J. C. Watts joined the BCS's payroll in 2003, he brought gravitas to the political and college football worlds. After four consecutive terms as the U.S. Representative from Oklahoma's 4th District, Watts left the House to start a lobbying firm. His success running the University of Oklahoma's offense from 1979 to 1981 gave him credibility to a group that needed a Washington rainmaker.

Watts was known for his tough, fearless, trailblazing ways. He grew up impoverished in rural Oklahoma and was one of the first black students to integrate his elementary school. Originally the Sooners' seventh-string quarterback, Watts soon ascended to the top of the depth chart and led Barry Switzer's offense with panache. In 1994, running as a Republican, Watts won a seat in the House. He voted to impeach Bill Clinton, refused to join the Congressional Black Caucus, and responded to catcalls of "Uncle Tom" by labeling his critics "race-hustling poverty pimps." Watts never felt a need to apologize for what he believed.

Then the Cartel hired him. Between 2003 and 2010, the BCS paid $710,000 to Watts' lobbying firm, J.C. Watts Companies, according to the Center for Responsive Politics. It bought some political pull, if not Watts' public approval.

"I don't advise the BCS on whether they should or shouldn't have a playoff," he told *USA Today* in 2009, declining to take a stance on the issue. "I just kind of help them navigate getting through the hearings and what to expect and how to prepare themselves."

Expensive tour guides are a Washington staple, and it was inevitable college football would enter the netherworld of profiteers who subsist off confusion, conflict, and coarse debate.

Political involvement draws lobbyists, and with billions of dollars in public money at stake—not to mention an easy way to gain the votes of impassioned fans—the politicians can't resist.

It isn't easy to shoo Congress away when the athletic departments of the ninety-nine public schools in Division I-A needed a combined $826 million in subsidies just to balance their books in 2008, according to *USA Today*. The number rose 20 percent the last three years, and it's not going to stop. If the system wants to waste taxpayer money, it can't easily complain when politicians start asking where it went. Good idea or not, Washington is now forever involved.

The political movement began in 2003 when Tulane president Scott Cowen, eyeing an annual $7 million budget shortfall in his athletic department, announced he would consider dropping his school's football team to Division III. Tulane fans decried the idea and some called for Cowen's ouster. Wisely, he retreated and instead found a common enemy.

Tulane had gone undefeated in 1998, and a spot in a lucrative BCS bowl would have cured its financial ills. As a member of Conference USA, Tulane had no access to the BCS bowls, even with an 11-0 record. Tulane settled for a Liberty Bowl appearance, and five years later, Cowen drew on the lingering resentment.

He organized forty-four of the fifty-two other non-BCS schools and set out on a media blitz to destroy the BCS. In an op-ed piece published by the *New York Times*, Cowen called on school presidents "to actively challenge the NCAA, the BCS, and the current system of intercollegiate athletics in this country." The non-BCS schools threatened legal action, arguing the postseason system violated antitrust laws. They persuaded influential congressmen to hold hearings on the matter.

Myles Brand, the late president of the NCAA, sprung to mediate the issue. He was adamant that colleges needed to re-

solve their matters without interference from "external parties."
He helped forge a new deal in which the six BCS conferences
shared some revenue with the smaller conferences and created
a road map for access to BCS bowls and even the title game. The
politicians were held at bay.

The Cartel kept its tentacles in Washington anyway. Hogan
& Hartson, a D.C.-based law firm that specializes in lobbying,
joined the BCS payroll in 2003. "Throughout the world," the
company's Web site reads, "government investigators are step-
ping up antitrust enforcement." Where Watts could not reach,
Hogan & Hartson would.

That same year, the non-BCS schools hired Edelman, a well-
known public-relations firm, to polish their message of injustice
in Washington. And though Brand's compromise involved increased access, it wasn't enough for the Mountain West. In
2009, it broke ranks and spent $250,000 to hire its own law
firm, Arent Fox, which is arguing that the BCS violates antitrust laws because "competitors cannot, by acting together and
with the primary distributors in a market, impose market re-
straints that guarantee that regardless of the quality of their
products, they will receive the vast majority of market revenues
and market access. Yet that is exactly what has occurred here
under the BCS."

Individual schools did their part, too. Purdue and the University of Michigan spent more than $900,000 in lobbying fees,
according to federal filings, and one of their objectives was to
oppose a BCS bill. The ACC and NCAA combined to spend another $370,000 on lobbyists who pressed the issue.

The opposition joined in last year as well. Playoff PAC, a
federal political-action committee designed to undermine the
BCS, became a go-to voice whenever politicians engaged in BCS
saber rattling. Created by six football fans in their twenties and

thirties—including Matthew Sanderson, a former campaign finance counsel to Sen. John McCain's presidential campaign—
Playoff PAC is a part-time endeavor of bipartisan unity, both
politically and in the organizers' fandom.

"We have two University of Utah fans, one BYU fan, one
University of Texas fan and one USC fan," Sanderson said. "I
don't know who [the sixth member] is a fan of. I think he's just
against the BCS on principle. Our organization was created to
ratchet up policy and public pressure to change college football."

The fight in Washington is on, ever more money spent on a
quandary with a workable resolution. Of course, that needs to
start in the back rooms where the Cartel figures out where to
take college football next. And right now, the power brokers are
too busy gerrymandering their futures to even know.

In 2009, the Mountain West not only refused to sign a pend-
ing BCS television deal with ESPN/ABC, commissioner Craig
Thompson publicly opposed the system in appearances on Capitol Hill. It was a bold act of revolution. And it went over poorly
with the big and small conferences.

The Western Athletic Conference remains miffed that the
Mountain West took such bold steps rather than work inside the
system. It didn't help when the Mountain West swiped the WAC's
breadwinner, Boise State, to bulk up in 2011 and try to secure
its place as a conference with an automatic qualification for a BCS
bowl game. Make no mistake: For that enormous cut of BCS
money, the Mountain West and WAC would surely leave behind
the Sun Belt, Mid-American, and Conference USA, which are
happy to take the yearly BCS handout Brand helped negotiate for
them.

While each of the big six conferences received at least $19.8

million from last year's BCS pool, the Mountain West cashed in just $9.8 million. The WAC earned $7.8 million. The conferences without a team in a BCS game took their payouts—$2.8 million for Conference USA, $2.1 million for the MAC, and $1.5 million for the Sun Belt—and spent another year hoping for a playoff and the $25 million it could guarantee.

The payoffs, particularly to the smallest conferences, amount to hush money—or at least they were supposed to, until Thompson aired his grievances and took public a sliver of the infighting that plagues the BCS.

"I was very disturbed [that] any of our conferences that are part of the BCS [came] out after we negotiated with television and then [proposed] drastic changes to the system," Big 12 commissioner Dan Beebe told the *Dallas Morning News*. "The Mountain West acts like we're holding a gun to their head."

In the wake of all the consternation, tension has increased at the BCS meetings. Factions draw lines and use their political heft to intimidate. "This past year I was out of the room a lot as they discussed me," Thompson said. "I spent more time in the hallway, like a sixth grader."

He wouldn't apologize. He can't. The Mountain West had one BCS team in 2009, Texas Christian. So did the ACC, Big East, Big 12, and Pac-10. The major conferences received nearly $10 million more anyway. One of the Mountain West's attorneys, Alan Fishel, released a chart that showed teams from the Mountain West and WAC bought more tickets and produced higher television ratings for their BCS bowl appearances than teams from the ACC or Big East, yet they received half the revenue. Hancock likes to claim the BCS is primarily about getting the No. 1 and No. 2 teams to meet in bowl game. It's clearly more than that. The inequity forces the Mountain West to do what it can to change the system, Thompson said, while "if you're one of the six automatic qualifying conferences, you don't."

Unless you're Mike Slive. Or John Swofford. Or, really, anyone. Thompson is wrong: Every member of the Cartel will try to change the system if it behooves his conference. Which is why, amid the internal infighting and mixed messages, it brought on Hancock. Along with Fleischer's guidance, he could ensure the BCS presented a united front and stayed on message.

Soon after he was hired, Hancock made a round of media appearances. Somewhere along the way, he must have lost his cue cards. When he joined the hosts of Atlanta's *Mayhem in the AM* radio show in November 2009, Hancock was asked if even he, the official head of the BCS, liked the BCS.

"You know," Hancock said, "I like the plus-one, personally. That's a four-team playoff."

17 Implicit Trust, Explicit Motivations

Pac-10 commissioner Larry Scott was circling the South Plains in a Raytheon Hawker 800 twin-engine jet like a buzzard about to pick apart what was expected to be the carcass of the Big 12 conference. Colorado already had seceded to the Pac-10. Nebraska had left for the Big Ten. Few thought the league would last another forty-eight hours. It was June 13, 2010, a Sunday, and Scott was puddle jumping from city to city, offering personal invitations to Texas, Texas Tech, Oklahoma, Oklahoma State, and Texas A&M to join the new Pac-16. It would be the first superconference, one that would stretch some 2,500 miles and link cultures as different as the dueling pronunciations and definitions of rodeo. Out west, it's a swanky street with an accent. Down south, it's a sport with a twang.

When Tom Hansen retired as commissioner of the Pac-10 in 2009, the league replaced him with Scott, a college sports outsider who had previously run the Women's Tennis Association. He surveyed his new property, wondered how a conference that owned almost the entire West Coast lagged so far behind in revenue, and set out to fix it. Within months, the league's presidents empowered Scott to build a superconference—a profound assault on Hansen's archaic vision of college athletics.

Scott immediately targeted Texas, one of the most storied programs in the country, a revenue behemoth, and, most important, an entrée into an unbeatable market. With the Longhorns in the south and Trojans out west anchoring a Pac-16 television network, the conference would reap money from the country's two most populous states and a projected 30 million–plus total households. Among the Cartel's heavy hitters, Scott looked like the ultimate leviathan: Within a year of taking over the Pac-10, he was puppeteer for the future of college football.

It took a consortium to cut his strings. As the Pac-10 readied to cause upheaval, a group of athletic officials, politicians, and boosters agreed this was happening too fast, that the departure of Texas and the other Big 12 schools would needlessly destroy a conference whose history dated back to the formation of the Big Six in 1907. The prospect of four superconferences—the Pac-16, plus sixteen-team versions of the Big Ten, ACC, and SEC—made perfect sense to outsiders such as Scott. He did what any smart businessman would: chase and acquire the most valuable asset. His hold on Texas simply wasn't strong enough.

That the Big 12 nearly died because of the Pac-10 and the Big Ten was an irony not lost on those who watched Big 12 commissioner Dan Beebe nearly oversee his conference's extinction. They were the two leagues with which Beebe aligned two years earlier to torpedo SEC commissioner Mike Slive's plus-one plan. Beebe never saw that the need for diversified revenue streams was paramount to stopping this very sort of calamity. And only a face-saving 11th-hour agreement promising Texas a disproportionate cut of conference revenue and the ability to build its own TV network convinced the school to turn down the Pac-10 invitation and save the Big 12—for now. Though Scott flew home without any other schools, the threat of expansion remains in part because Beebe, former Big East commissioner Mike Tranghese, and their presidents weren't wise enough to see the threat coming.

After the commissioners committed first-degree homicide

on Slive's playoff presentation, Big Ten commissioner Jim Delany conceded that the plus-one would have succeeded. He opposed it nonetheless. Delany is unapologetic in saying his interests are what's best for the Big Ten and the Big Ten only. His business acumen revolutionized the sport. Current Big East commissioner John Marinatto has called him Gordon Gekko, who lived by an ethos: Greed is good. The only curious part: That a man so integral in building the Big Ten into a financial giant would so blithely turn down piles of money provided by a playoff.

Delany did so by following a simple Big Ten principle: The best offense is often a great defense, and he needed to protect his conference's power base. More important than raising all of college football's revenues was maintaining the revenue gap between the Big Ten and everyone else. The cause of that chasm: television contracts. Never mind that Illinois ($4.5 million), Wisconsin ($3.4 million), and Minnesota ($3.4 million) used general university funds to balance their athletic department budgets, money that would be more than covered by a playoff bounty. As long as the future of college football was tied to TV, the Big Ten's position on top of the revenue mountain was assured.

With around 26 percent of the nation's homes in its traditional Midwest footprint, name-brand schools, and huge, passion-filled fan bases, the Big Ten can make a television deal like no other conference. Add on Delany's stroke-of-genius Big Ten Network, which garners a per-home rate of up to 70 cents a month from basic cable subscribers in the Midwest—a Big Ten tax—and the revenue gap widens.

Not even the SEC can keep up. While official figures are not released, the Big Ten hands out an estimated $20 million annually per school, a number expected to grow as the Big Ten Network gains traction. Even with its fifteen-year, $3 billion deal, the SEC doles out $15 million to $17 million to each university. The Big 12 runs between $7 million and $12 million, with marquee teams Texas, Oklahoma, and Texas A&M set to receive closer to Big Ten–level money for not leaving the conference. The Pac-10, with a 20 million–household area once Colorado and Utah arrive in 2011, could get a bump in its next deal. The ACC, thanks to a new ESPN contract, will dish out $12 million to $14 million per school. The Big East still trail significantly and most likely always will.

If the plus-one ever expanded, a pile of money worth hundreds of millions of dollars would be divvied up based on who wins actual games. And were playoff revenue to equal or exceed television money, it would threaten the Big Ten's stranglehold on the system. A playoff might be an on-field boon for the Big Ten. Or it might not. Either way, there would be two trails to the money, not one. And if you're Jim Delany, the last thing you want to do is risk that.

So what do you do? Find a way to stop even the most modest playoff.

For Delany, money is power, only in a bizarro way: The less money available to all, the more power stays with the Big Ten. By blocking a real postseason—and getting other leagues to foolishly oblige—the Big Ten has assured itself the biggest haul from a smaller treasure. It also means that it can pillage the Big 12, Big East, and ACC almost at will if it chooses to expand—which is why Nebraska quickly jumped and Missouri all but begged for an invitation that didn't arrive.

Along those lines, the BCS serves the Big Ten well. The at-large BCS selection process is based on the promise of ticket sales and television ratings, not necessarily on-field success. Over the past decade the Big Ten has received the most BCS bowl bids, seventeen, two more than the SEC. That the league went 6-11 in those games hasn't slowed momentum. In each of the last five years, it received the maximum of two teams per year. For the Big Ten that means more money and more exposure than the other leagues—even if the total payout compared to a playoff is fractional. The Big East and ACC didn't receive a single at-large slot over the last decade. The BCS fits into the Big Ten's starve-the-competitors business model.

The only reason the Big 12 and Big East should've opposed Slive's plus-one plan in 2008 is because it wasn't ambitious enough. Those conferences can never generate the league-wide television revenue to keep their members from wanting to run to the Big Ten. A real playoff is the only way to close the money gap, a gusher begging to be tapped.

Consider the 2008–09 season, where Big 12 members Oklahoma, Texas, and Texas Tech all would've been selected for our 16-team playoff. If the seeds held, those teams would've combined to play nine playoff games, earning nine $25 million shares for a total of $225 million. The conference then could've written each league school an $18.75 million check just from the playoff. That year, the Big Ten, featuring playoff-bound Ohio State and Penn State competing in three games, would've earned $75 million, a per-team share of $6.8 million. The nearly $12 million more in playoff money would've evened the Big 12 with the Big Ten, negating the TV imbalance. Nebraska, in that case, no longer would've had a revenue reason to bail on the league.

Beebe, Tranghese, and their presidents never saw the plus-one for what it was: not a postseason plan but a lifeline for long-term survival. Without it, they're forever susceptible to destruction, leaving proud and successful athletic departments such as Kansas, Kansas State, Missouri, Baylor, Iowa State, Syracuse, West Virginia, Louisville, Cincinnati, Connecticut, and others dealing with threats based on demographics, economics, and geography instead of football and basketball relevance. If you're associated with one of those schools and not pushing for a playoff, you're hopelessly naïve to reality.

In that case, Beebe might be the ideal leader. Even as Delany studied expansion throughout the first half of 2010, Beebe kept publicly declaring him a trusted friend. He dismissed worries by fans that the Big Ten was covertly negotiating with Big 12 schools.

"I expect that Jim, who I have known for many, many years and trust implicitly, [will] do what he said he's going to do," Beebe said. "If and when the time comes that they're going to do anything—and if that includes any of the institutions in the Big 12—he'll let me know first."

A few hours before Nebraska announced its intention to seek membership with the Big Ten, Beebe said, Delany called him to break the news. The Big Ten and Nebraska had been talking for a month, school officials later said. *The Columbus Dispatch* printed e-mails between Ohio State president E. Gordon Gee and Delany dating back to April that discussed Gee courting Texas to join the league.

So much for Mr. Implicit Trust.

As irresponsible obstinacy goes, former Pac-10 commissioner Tom Hansen's rejoinder to Slive's plus-one plan remains a Picasso. Mere mention of the plus-one triggered Hansen's fight-or-flight reaction, and one day, against all reason, he threatened to take his ball and go home.

"It's a little annoying that my colleagues continue to float this idea as though it has merit," Hansen told Matt Hayes of *The Sporting News* prior to Slive's presentation. "If they continue to push it, and try to push us into a corner . . ."

BORDERS.

BOOKS MUSIC MOVIES CAFE

ALL SALES FINAL
NO RETURNS/EXCHANGES

STORE: 0529   REG: 01/02   TRAN#: 6142
LE   03/12/201   EMP: 05053

ATH TO BCS
    3143982   CL T   14.00
  20.00 30% PROMO
RE THAN WINNING
    9892858   QP T   11.86
  16.95 30% PROMO

              Subtotal   25.86
              MISSOURI 7 %   1.97
  Items   Total   27.83
              MASTERCARD   27.83
CT # /S XXXXXXXXXXXXX7 6
                 AUTH: 110711
E: GARRISON/NICHOLA F

CUSTOMER COPY

ou Saved $11.09

       03/12/2011   :05AM
NS BARCODE: 052901 420505303121

ALL SALES FINAL

Thank you for you patronage.

Well, Hansen implied, the Pac-10 might have to pull out of the BCS. The mess he helped create was a worthwhile mess until it started assaulting the traditions Hansen purported to hold so dear. His posturing reeked of desperation and futility; Hansen's ideals had all the modernity of a cotton gin. Had anyone called his bluff, he would have been fired before the first SEC recruiter landed at LAX to pounce on what instantly would have become an irrelevant conference. The Pac-10 needs the prospect of being able to compete for the national championship, however screwy the system, and Hansen grossly overestimated his power if he believed USC, Oregon, and the remaining Pac-10 schools would relinquish that opportunity.

Part of the Cartel, however, embraced Hansen's brazen attitude. The threat: Keep complaining about the BCS, and we'll take the entire sport back to the old bowl system, where certain leagues had contractual tie-ins to certain bowls. "The only alternative is to return to the old bowl system that operated from 1902 until 1991," Nebraska chancellor Harvey Perlman testified to Congress in July 2009.

This is like the child that threatens to run away to protest an early bedtime. Go ahead, son, and be sure to call from the end of the driveway. A return to the old bowl system would be lunacy, economic suicide too absurd to even discuss if Perlman hadn't said it on Capitol Hill and other Cartel members hadn't repeated it since.

The Cartel can take the bowl system back to the 1980s. It just can't take expenditures back to the 1980s, which makes the entire threat idle. They may have played college football in the 1980s, but they didn't pay head coaches $5 million (Texas's Mack Brown), athletic directors $4 million (Kansas's Lew Perkins), or defensive coordinators $1 million (USC's Monte Kiffin). They didn't have $50 million practice facilities or quarter-billion-dollar stadium renovations. In 1991, the University of Florida's athletic budget was about $24.1 million, or $37.5 million in 2010 dollars. The school approved $96.4 million for its 2010–11 budget.

In the '80s, the Cartel didn't have thirty-five bowl games that needed subsidization. There were nineteen, and they were self-sufficient. Leagues didn't stretch across vast regions of the country, causing field hockey travel costs to spike. Schools still thought twice about dropping millions buying out a failed coach and his staff.

The BCS is a weak, outdated system. The old one was even weaker and more outdated.

It's one thing for a sport that needs more funding to turn down hundreds of millions from a playoff. It's another to commit such a nose-cutting, face-spiting blunder as slashing revenue. Presuming the Big Ten and Pac-10 stuck with the Rose Bowl, the SEC went with the Sugar, the Big 12 linked up with the Fiesta, and the ACC married the Orange Bowl, it would be virtually impossible to create the No. 1 vs. No. 2 matchup that demands so much money. During the 1980s, a number of major independent programs (Penn State, Miami, Florida State) allowed the occasional title game to form. Today, only Notre Dame remains a potential power without a league. Pre-BCS, the top-tier bowl games often would feature one league champion against another conference's second-place team. Under current membership status, the above scenario wouldn't have produced a single 1-2 game during the BCS era.

Currently, the BCS receives $125 million a year in TV money for four games: the championship, Fiesta, Orange, and Sugar. The Rose Bowl has its own $30 million deal, which would continue relatively unabated, television executives believe. The other BCS bowls would suffer, payouts decreasing accordingly.

The four-game BCS deal is predicated on the ratings bump

the championship game delivers. In 2010, the title game drew a 17.2 Nielsen rating, while the other BCS bowls averaged a 7.8. The money is in the big game and only the big game. The other bowls are simply pooled together to create stability. BCS pay-outs, subsequently, reach close to $20 million per team, even for a low-rated, sparsely attended Orange Bowl.

The old bowl system kills the possibility of a 1-2 title game, the supposed impetus behind the BCS in the first place. There would be just three games to sell, not four. Take away the guar-anteed game between Nos. 1 and 2 and television revenue dries up. A panel of current and retired television executives esti-mated the contracts would drop from an average of $31 million per game to between $10 million and $15 million. That $125 million deal would become $45 million, just 36 percent of the old money. And that's the high end of the estimate.

Gone, in that scenario, are the subsidies that keep the mid- and low-tier bowl games alive. If the Fiesta Bowl can't provide enough revenue to the Big 12 for the league to handle the inevi-table losses from the Insight Bowl, the Insight Bowl will die. De-funct, then, is the bowl system as we know it. Bowl executives estimate just fourteen games could survive without the BCS bail-out money. With his threat, Perlman illustrated how all the mem-bers of the Cartel operate: looking out for themselves and only themselves. In the name of preserving the bowl system, Perlman threatened to kill it, without either concern or a clue about what he was actually saying.

Not all BCS games would fare the same, either, which ought to terrify Marinatto, the Big East commissioner. Instead, he too has casually floated the doomsday old bowl system idea. Ac-cording to television executives, the Sugar Bowl, with its SEC ties, could still attract a $20 million TV deal. An Orange Bowl anchored by the ACC might get only $6 million annually. If so, the ACC's big payout could drop to the $4 million range. The Big East, without a tie-in, would struggle to get invited to any of the former BCS bowls. The old system would allow for just three at-large spots. The competition would include not just Notre Dame or a Mountain West power but a second- or even third-place team from the Big Ten, Big 12, Pac-10, or SEC. Bowl executives care about potential ticket sales and television ratings, not the fairness of the selection process.

The old system would decimate the Big East, eliminating its BCS calling card in recruiting and potentially bankrupting some of its athletic departments. Every conference would suffer from a regression to the 1980s; the Big East would fare worst of all. Cincinnati went to consecutive BCS games, and its athletic department still wound up with a $24 million debt. To balance its books, Rutgers hit up students, taxpayers, and the school's general funds to cover $22.1 million in fiscal 2008, according to *USA Today*. South Florida received $12.9 million in university subsidies and Connecticut $11.2 million to stay afloat. Without BCS money, they would need millions more. A playoff would lead to collectively prosperity; a return to the old system offers widespread poverty.

Yet Jim Delany somehow found accomplices to go against their leagues' interests and block discussion of the plus-one. And it would surprise no one if Larry Scott formulated a new raid, fueled up his jet, and pointed it back at the Lone Star State to prove the superconference is the way of college football's future.

Remember, everything will be fine. Just trust them.

18 Death to the BCS

Of the myriad issues on the 2008 presidential campaign, nothing brought together Barack Obama and John McCain quite like college football. They could argue. They could debate. They could sneer. And in the end, their disdain for the BCS remained a shared value.

"Fed up with it," Obama said.

"I'm very unhappy with the BCS," McCain said.

It wasn't simply a campaign-trail issue, either. By 2010, a rural Texas Republican (Joe Barton) and a former Black Panther Democrat from Chicago (Bobby Rush) were cooperating to hold hearings and cosponsor legislation in a House subcommittee.

Meanwhile, the Democratic Department of Justice considered pursuing an antitrust investigation against the BCS after Republican senator Orrin Hatch of Utah urged an inquiry.

"The notion of basic fairness is called into question by the current BCS system," Hatch said. "I believe there is value to ensuring fairness in our society whenever we can. And while life may not be fair, the moment that we stop caring that it isn't, we chip away at the American Dream."

Conservative columnist George Will declared the BCS "unfair." Democratic strategist James Carville said it was "borderline criminal."

Left and right, black and white, a virtual rainbow coalition lined up to take its whacks. Opposition to the BCS is so deep and pervasive it has solved one of the country's biggest problems: divisive politics. There's nothing like universal disgust to bridge the aisle, even in Washington.

"Bipartisanship lives," Will wrote.

Of the offended, only Carville is publicly a hardcore college football loyalist, LSU his school of choice. They are politicians, though, and they sense not just the 90 percent disapproval of the BCS but a conflict with the core values that define the country. How the Cartel runs college football isn't simply wrong.

The BCS is un-American.

It steps on the upstart. It discriminates. It dictates who plays, and if any opposition arises, the men in charge dismiss it. College football is not the land of the free and the home of the brave. It is the land of Beef 'O' Brady's and the home of Papajohns.com.

We want fairness, a level playing field, a chance. Individuals rising to fulfill unknown potential. Teams proving their sum greater than their parts. *Rocky* and *Rudy* and *Miracle* and *Hoosiers*. It's the ability to compete no matter where you come from, no matter how few believe in you. It's the magic of sports.

Too many times in our lives, the American ideal doesn't occur. There are no level playing fields in business, little fairness in government. We're desperate for it in sports because it's still possible, this place where everyone is allowed the opportunity to win fair and square. The Cartel neuters what should be a crazed November, an even more important round of conference-title games, and a brilliant December and January worth of meaningful postseason football. Any sport without a playoff to determine its champion is hardly a sport at all.

"We have playoffs in every sport in the world except college football," South Carolina coach Steve Spurrier said. "How can we be right and everybody else wrong?"

College football is perhaps the most American pastime. It's played at the highest level in forty-one states, in cities big and small, from Los Angeles to Las Cruces, Miami to Madison. If a school wants to be great, it can overcome geography, weather, and wealth. Nebraska, home of 1.8 million people who proudly call themselves Cornhuskers, is a historic powerhouse. Iowa and West Virginia regularly field teams capable of beating anyone. Oregon hosts a pair of perennial Top 25 teams. For a stretch, the hottest program in the country operated out of dusty Lubbock, Texas. Two of the last four BCS titles were won by a team from such a remote, landlocked spot in northern Florida its stadium is nicknamed "The Swamp." And that's a term of endearment.

The romance missing in professional sports still exists in college football, and no place stokes it quite like the Rose Bowl. The stadium turned eighty-eight in 2010, and though the wear of age is undeniable, so is the atmosphere at the annual New Year's Day game. The sun crests over the San Gabriel Mountains, and the evening air tastes like a stick of sugar cane, and 100,000 people migrate to Pasadena, a city away from the bustle of Los Angeles, for the most historic football game there is. The whole thing is kissed by something divine.

"We're ingrained in America," said Mitch Dorger, the recently retired Rose Bowl CEO. "We've been going on for four generations. We represent something special. It's something a big part of the country looks forward to—seeing that game."

And right now, it's just a BCS game. One first played in 1902, more than thirty years before the Sugar Bowl and Orange Bowl and Sun Bowl commenced, and one with oodles of memories on top of its charm, but a game with meaning limited in scope. The marriage of the Rose Bowl and the title game of our sixteen-team playoff, on the other hand, brings the ultimate significance to the ultimate game.

Imagine: The Rose Bowl National Championship Game, an

officially sanctioned, BCS-free culmination of a season unshack-led from the Cartel. The proper way to dignify the most impor-tant bowl is by making it more important, and the best way to make the Rose Bowl more important is by giving it the national championship every season instead of once in four years.

"We'd love to sign up for it if we were asked to," Dorger said.

So would the other BCS bowls. Seeing as the Fiesta Bowl's CEO allegedly set up a massive campaign-contribution scheme, it's out. While the Orange Bowl enjoys longevity and location, it couldn't sell out last year's game, and Sun Life Stadium simply doesn't carry the grand setting a title game deserves. The Sugar Bowl is a worthy host, with its past, its stadium, and its reputa-tion, though its ability to grab the top non-playoff team out of the SEC would keep it plenty relevant without a championship.

Pasadena would become college football's version of Omaha, the site of baseball's College World Series for the last sixty years. Everything would lead there, from the first games in September to the three previous playoff rounds held in campus stadiums. It would restore the sense of impermeability the Rose Bowl Game held before it sold out and cemented the formation of the BCS. Nevertheless, the Rose Bowl, the place, lived on, and for history, aesthetics, and grandeur, nothing beats it.

Even an old Ohio State fan like Dorger, who grew up in Columbus at the altar of Woody Hayes, sees the allure of Pasa-dena hosting the national-title game. No longer is the Rose Bowl an exclusive arrangement between the Big Ten and Pac-10, and so all of the great teams it missed throughout the years could now play there, and for a recognized title, no less.

"It's great to have a storied program like an Oklahoma or Texas or Alabama come out to the Rose Bowl," Dorger said, and, barring upsets—which wouldn't be such a bad thing, really—that would happen every year.

That's the thing about the proposed sixteen-team playoff: It doesn't create problems, it solves them. It grows the best of the sport while maintaining long-held traditions. It encourages the upstart and welcomes anyone. It is, above all, fair. Lost in the Cartel's myopia is the good of the game, the wants of the participants, the will of the fans, replaced by divergent interests, self-serving arguments, inconsequential money grabs, and petty power plays.

In a sport so grand, the leadership is so small. It's depressing to witness up close.

A few men control everything, and if ever anyone wondered why a cartel is dangerous, college football exhibits it. The BCS suppresses competition and cheats a sport out of possible history-making games. It's not just the underdogs, either. The best teams covet the chance to take on all challengers, to knock off a nation full of playoff foes and prove their lofty, heavyweight reputation. The great rivalries are when the best of the best face off: Lakers-Celtics, Yankees–Red Sox, Carolina-Duke.

The BCS supplies neither. After dismissing the small-conference teams with a collective chuckle, the Cartel then prevents the in crowd from enjoying a playoff ride and offers instead one-off bowl games and pats on the back.

Well, we prefer more football to congratulatory wishes. Like, say, Penn State at Florida. Or LSU traveling to unbeaten Texas Christian. Both would have been first-round games last year under our playoff, which, like the wildly popular and profitable NCAA men's basketball tournament, provides automatic bids to the champions of all conferences (eleven in football) and fills the rest of the spots with at-large teams chosen by a selection committee (another five).

Though it seems counterintuitive to invite the Sun Belt champion to a playoff that determines the national title, the presence of the underdog accomplishes plenty. First is inclusion. In every other sport, a team—any team—can start the season with a clear goal: win every game, and it's champion. By offering access to anyone, all antitrust threats vanish, and the possibility of a low seed upsetting one of the nation's best teams tingles the spine. Appalachian State beating Michigan in a 2007 regular-season game still resonates. The magnitude of such a game in the post-season would be immeasurable.

Involving weaker teams actually rewards the strongest with a near-guarantee of a first-round victory, a competitive advantage three months of regular-season excellence in the making. In 2009, seeding teams based on the final BCS standings, No. 1 Alabama would earn a game against No. 16 Troy. SEC runner-up Florida, a fifth seed, would draw No. 12 Penn State. It's a big difference, and it makes every game of the regular season—or, in this case, the SEC title game—matter.

Home-field advantage through the first three rounds of the playoffs incentivizes the regular season even more. The opportunity to play at a familiar stadium, in front of a rabid crowd, for as long as possible, would turn the chase for high seeds into an all-out November brawl. Yet the NFL playoffs prove that road teams can win: the New York Giants did it three times to reach the 2008 Super Bowl, where they beat undefeated New England at a neutral site.

Putting the playoffs on campus would energize intraregional rivalries, drawing Pac-10 teams to SEC stadiums, putting powerhouses on Boise State's blue turf, and bringing weather and wild crowds back into the fray. Had all the top seeds of the 2009 tournament won, the second-round matchups would have unfolded as follows: Ohio State at Alabama, defending national champion Florida traveling to unbeaten Texas Christian, Oregon visiting Texas, and the battle of two perfect teams, Boise State at Cincinnati.

It stirs the imagination of anyone who loves football, and it works brilliantly. The four playoff weekends could take place over the last two weekends of December and the first two of January, precisely the time frame of the current bowl calendar. Playoff teams would have between a two- and three-week break from the end of their seasons and the playoffs, time to heal, recharge, and study.

The first weekend would be college football's equivalent to the action-packed opening days of the men's basketball tournament, the perfect excuse to play hooky from work and permanently dent the couch cushion. The next Saturday, the winners play at the higher seed's home stadium. Same for the semifinals. And finally the championship, which, in the 2010–11 season, would take place on the exact day as the BCS title game. Players would miss minimal class time. Practices, which already take place under the bowl system during finals, would not change.

Teams in the championship game would play sixteen or seventeen games. While the health of the players is imperative, the conference commissioners long ago lost any moral standing or practical credibility on it. Players practice fifteen times after the season for bowl games and for another month prior to the spring game. They play in conference title games created for the money and travel longer distances because conference expansion meant more cash. Most egregious, the Cartel extended the regular season in recent years from eleven games to twelve—a net gain of 120 teams playing an extra sixty minutes—which affects far more players than a playoff, where only eight teams would play more than under the bowl system.

Never mind that in many states a high school team, with stars playing both ways, requires sixteen-game seasons from its champions. Or that in the NFL, with fifty-three-man rosters, players participate in as many as twenty-four games from pre-season to Super Bowl.

If the Cartel worries about player safety, let it adopt the NFL's game clock, which doesn't stop after each first down. Much like how in baseball pitch count matters more than innings pitched, it isn't the number of games that cause injuries in football but the number of snaps. College games contain from 8 to 10 percent more plays (even before its prolonged overtime), making the fourteen-game college season equivalent to fifteen NFL games.

With a playoff, the health of conferences big and small would improve drastically. Tournament berths would spark interest in fringe programs. Making seasons matter more in the Mid-American Conference or Conference USA is a net positive. No longer would a team from a smaller conference have the possibility of riding weak competition directly to the championship game. Everyone, big and small, would have to earn it the way Butler did in men's basketball.

All six major conferences would receive at least one bid, allowing a league championship to matter even more in such conferences as the ACC and Big East. The race for those automatic bids would draw national interest and drive TV ratings for regular-season and conference title-game action. With five at-large bids going most years to the big six conferences, they would still represent the vast majority of teams. Notre Dame or a second Mountain West or WAC team would compete for a chance to play also, neither aided nor penalized by perception or earning power.

While BCS executive director Bill Hancock frets over the hurt feelings of the last fan base left out, the selection committee would choose among flawed teams, not arbitrarily deny undefeated ones. Going by the 2009 BCS standings—perhaps one consideration for the committee, though certainly not the only one—9-3 LSU would've edged 10-2 BYU for the final bid. The Cougars would have no legitimate complaint. They lost twice. Anyway, their consolation prize: a trip to one of the former BCS bowl games to play another strong opponent.

The bowls would remain in business and fill much of the December calendar with good football. They're fun events and, despite the one-sided business deals and abject money-wasting college football should've long ago addressed, there are worse fates than having them remain—as long as it's not as sites for the playoff games. The bowls' missions require teams and their fans to come and spend money for nearly a week, something that wouldn't occur with a playoff. If true to their stated goals of serving as a community-driven event that attracts out-of-town visitors to boost economic impact, bowls would stay far from the tournament.

Bowl season would continue as long as the Cartel wanted to fund it. Our panel of television executives, athletic directors, commissioners, and marketing experts say the bowls would see enough of a reduction in revenue to cause a cut in bowl payouts of perhaps 30 percent. Doomsday scenario: The current $220 million that bowls pay to schools will be halved to $110 million—still enough to cover the bowls' costs and turn a profit while the sport bathes in playoff cash.

In the end, money—and who keeps the majority of it— drives the Cartel's actions. And how it can see the unbalanced budgets and taxpayer- and student-funded subsidies and not immediately gravitate toward a playoff suggests the worst sort of selfishness.

Our panel of television executives predicted a sixteen-team playoff would fetch as much as $600 million, although we'll take a more conservative estimate of $450 million. "This becomes a major, major television property," one executive said. "The title game alone is a $100 million property."

Then there are tickets, which, unlike with bowl games, would sell out in seconds—no visiting-school guarantee necessary. Using 2009 as a model, and including a title game at the Rose Bowl, the playoff would have approximately 1.2 million tickets to sell. Athletic administrators who studied our plan say the average price would be as high as $200 a seat, although a more conservative $150 would still net the playoff $180 million.

Marketing—from title sponsors to on-field advertisements— would add another $120 million, according to Glenn Wong, an expert on college athletics and former dean of the University of Massachusetts School of Sports Management. And this doesn't address the ancillary money. Schools that host games would see parking, concessions, and stadium signage worth millions fall into their lap. Every school could charge boosters and season-ticket holders a premium for the right to purchase coveted play-off tickets for home games and even more coveted travel packages and tickets for road games. It wouldn't matter if a team makes the playoffs. Just the hope would increase donations.

Using conservative estimates on television, tickets, and marketing, a sixteen-team playoff would gross $750 million. Its popularity would unquestionably grow, and nearly every expert surveyed said a playoff's revenues could exceed $1 billion within five years.

The $750 million alone is an obscene sum for college sports, dwarfing even the men's basketball tournament. The money would be divided simply: Every time a team plays a game, its conference gets one share. With fifteen games, the booty is cut thirty ways, each appearance worth $25 million. If the system wants to kick in a million or two extra for the host team to cover costs, so be it. For now, we'll stick with the round $25 million number.

Were the highest seeds to advance in the 2009–10 tournament, the SEC alone would have grossed $175 million. After expenses, it likely would profit more than all of college football does in the current bowl system. The Big Ten and Big 12 would have earned $100 million each. And for the Mid-American or Conference USA, a single slice of the $25 million share would more than fund some teams' entire football budgets.

The big six conferences would still get the overwhelming share of the money, 73.3 percent of it, or $550 million, in 2009–10. The previous season, the big six leagues would have gotten 76.7 percent of the money. That year, the Big 12 alone would have earned nine shares, or $225 million. If getting around three-quarters of the massive revenue isn't enough for the Cartel, surely it can explain itself to Congress.

Getting college football's leaders to wake up, step up, and bring the game up is, of course, the difficult part. Entrenched egos are never easy to sway. Fear of change is oxygen to the status quo. Perhaps only the federal government, through the powerful Justice Department's pursuit of antitrust charges, can lessen the Cartel's grip. Or maybe it's something simpler: the confluence of fact finally rooting its way into the public domain, and that public demanding someone take action.

Upon his hiring as a media consultant for the Cartel, Ari Fleischer declared that for far too long playoff advocates haven't been forced to explain their alternative plan. Fleischer had it confused. The disorganization of the playoff crowd was the best thing to happen to the BCS. A unified plan built on considerable research and fresh perspectives should be the BCS's death knell.

Education can change everything. Questions can coerce action. University presidents need to examine the situation themselves, not be led around by their conference commissioners. Mark Emmert, the NCAA's new president who was formerly the president of the University of Washington, told the *Seattle Times* a playoff is "inevitable" and has expressed a willingness to work with campus leaders to understand the issues. A better understanding of the current wrong and potential right can cause momentum to shift and defenders of the system to shrivel. Fans, administrators, media, and presidents—all of whom have been force-fed conventional wisdom and unchallenged mistruths— must focus on what's real.

It's the Cartel that for far too long had it easy, allowed to spit arguments that carry no merit. Their decades-old talking points are built on false premises, their economics unsound, their antiquated system useless in a modern world they can't change, their bowl scheme bleeding schools dry while middlemen cash checks.

When presidents see what's really going on, and when the media learns the particulars of the system, and when fans clear the smoke screens, and when everyone collectively ignores misdirection and forces the Cartel to address the reality of its racket, and when the ideals espoused by Joe Paterno supplant those of Jim Delany—that's when the BCS falls like a house of cards.

And that's when players, coaches, and fans finally get the champion they deserve.

ACKNOWLEDGMENTS

In the course of conducting more than one hundred interviews for this book, we benefited from the perspective and patience of people throughout the world of college and professional sports. Pulling apart the Bowl Championship Series wasn't easy. Some people knew some things; others knew others. Almost no one had a firm grasp on all of the divergent and diverse interests that keep the BCS running against what's best for college football.

The experts helped us ferret out the depths of misinformation and misunderstanding. When presented with new information or perspectives, they were tremendous at unraveling not just the various scams but why they were in place. Understanding that this book may not be popular with many of the powerful (and vengeful) people in college athletics, we won't mention by name some of the most helpful to us, be they administrators, media, coaches, or television executives. That includes the many who took time to read the book in various forms and offer invaluable feedback. If asked, just pretend we've never met.

Since he fears no retribution, Ivan Glasser, the world's greatest CPA and most devout Michigan Wolverines fan, was a great resource in comprehending the fine print in so many financial documents.

Our agent, Jay Mandel of William Morris Endeavor, grasped

the enormous potential for this book and enthusiastically backed the project. His assistant, Jake Sugarman, has a bright future in the business.

In Patrick Mulligan at Gotham we found a New York editor who recognized the frustration college fans across the country have with the BCS. He then helped us craft the argument against it. Along with assistant Travers Johnson and publicist Beth Parker, he should be celebrated at every tailgate in America.

We owe a debt of gratitude to our bosses at Yahoo! Sports who not only allow us to rattle the cages of influence on a daily basis but stood strongly behind this book. They include Jimmy Pitaro, Dave Morgan, Kyle Laughlin, Joe Lago, Jon Baum, Gerry Ahern, and Steve Henson. Colleagues such as Adrian Wojnarowski, Charles Robinson, Jason King, and Al Toby were always there to lean on.

Dan Wetzel wants to thank his parents, Mary Ellen and Paul, as well as friends Brian Murphy, Paul Tryder, Matt Tryder, Gator Anderson, Pinky Wilson, Scott "Hawkeye" Hammer, Alex "Fightin' Irish" Clark, and Dan "Gator" Strickowski. Also, Bob Bronstein of the 24 Seconds bar in Berkley, Michigan. Most important is his beautiful wife, Jan, and young daughters Allie and Caitlin, who deal with the chaos his career creates—in this case, spending hours poring over aging tax returns.

Josh Peter wants to thank his incomparable wife, Vanessa, and their daughter, Norah, who, like it or not, are always part of the process, whether it be editing, cheerleading, or guiding.

And Jeff Passan wants to thank his ever-amazing wife, Sara, and son, Jack, who made sure to take extra-good care of him when he was pulling all-nighters. Debbie, Rich, and Nicole Passan: You are the best family possible. To Greg Bishop, Eli Saslow, Chico Harlan, Jon Bartner, Sonny Mazzolini, Wright

Thompson, Jill Mercadante, Joe Kanakaraj, Mike Vaccaro, Kevin Kaduk, Sam Mellinger, and, of course, Otto Rieke: Appreciate your eyeballs, suggestions, and friendship.

We couldn't have written this book without all of you. We're glad we wrote it with you.